CW00472858

They Gave The Crowd Plenty Fun

Dear Susan,

Best wishes and Thanks
for your Support!

Colin

Published by Hansib Publications in 2012
London and Hertfordshire

Hansib Publications Limited
P.O. Box 226, Hertford, Hertfordshire, SG14 3WY
United Kingdom

Email: info@hansib-books.com
Website: www.hansib-books.com

A catalogue record for this book is available from the British Library

ISBN 978-1-906190-55-2

Copyright © Colin Babb, 2012
Email: theygavethecrowd@hotmail.com
Facebook: They Gave The Crowd Plenty Fun
Flickr: http://www.flickr.com/photos/gavethecrowd/
Twitter: @gavethecrowd

All rights reserved. No part of this publication may be reproduced,
stored in or introduced into a retrieval system, or transmitted, in any
form, or by any means, electronic, mechanical, photocopying, recording
or otherwise, without the prior written permission of the publisher.

Design by Graphic Resolutions, Hertfordshire
Printed and bound in the UK

They Gave The Crowd Plenty Fun

*West Indian Cricket and its Relationship with
the British-Resident Caribbean Diaspora*

Colin Babb

Dedication

For my son, Nathan, an opening batsman in development.

This book is also dedicated to the staff and boys at the St. John Bosco Orphanage, Plaisance, East Coast Demerara, Guyana.

Contents

Author's Acknowledgements

Arif Ali, Shareef Ali and all at Hansib Publications.

Professor Trevor Burnard and Professor David Dabydeen for their inspiration and support for my work at The Yesu Persaud Centre for Caribbean Studies, University of Warwick. Some of the work I completed at Warwick has found its way into this book.

Yvonne Archer, Colin Grant, Julian Macho and Oliver Thornton for some practical advice and guidance about book publishing.

Sharon Devonish for her invaluable music research support.

Gavin Fuller, librarian at the Telegraph Media Group, for his invaluable newspaper research support.

Peter Lucas for his invaluable editorial recommendations and support.

Sharon Mendy, Secretary of Leeds Caribbean Cricket Club.

Jo Miller, Members' Liaison Officer at Surrey County Cricket Club, The Oval, for her invaluable photographic research support.

Martina Oliver at Getty Images.

John Partington for his invaluable audio research support.

All the helpful staff at The Bridgetown public library, Barbados.

Many thanks again to all the people who took time out to be interviewed and to share their thoughts, opinions and experiences:

Renee Babb, Honorary Secretary, Pickwick Cricket Club, Barbados.

Fabian Devlin, Head of Communications, Chance to Shine campaign.

Eaton Gordon, Deputy Sports Development Officer and Warwickshire Cricket Board Community Officer. Head Coach of Handsworth Cricket Club in Birmingham and Chance to Shine manager.

Ezekel Gray (The Man Ezeke), DJ, Entertainer and Musician. Writer and performer of 'Whose Grovelling Now?'

Rodney Hinds, Sports editor of The Voice newspaper, UK.

Colin Hutton, Former Crowd Control Police Sergeant at The Oval cricket ground.

Rohan Kallicharan, Cricket Columnist, Online Magazine Editor and Blogger.

Louis Mahoney, Actor and club cricketer.

Tony Moody, Cricket coach and Director of the Lambeth Cricket Academy, London.

Lord Bill Morris of Handsworth OJ, Independent Non-executive Director of the England and Wales Cricket Board (ECB).

Paul Morrison, Film director and writer of Wondrous Oblivion.

Mike Phillips, Academic, broadcaster and writer.

Earle Robinson, Cultural archivist and Leicester Caribbean Cricket Club trustee.

Professor Clem Seecharan, Head of Caribbean Studies at London Metropolitan University, academic and cricket writer.

Gladstone Small, Professional Cricketers' Association (PCA) ambassador. Former Warwickshire County Cricket Club and England player.

Steve Stephenson, Caribbean community leader, lecturer and Chairman of the Victoria Mutual Caribbean Cup cricket competition (UK).

Alex Tudor, Cricket coach: http://alextudor-coaching.com/
Former Surrey and Essex County Cricket Club and England player.

Paul Weekes, Cricket coach. Former Middlesex County Cricket Club player.

Harwood Williams, Chairman of the Leeds Caribbean Cricket Club.

Foreword

They Gave the Crowd Plenty Fun is a lucid and comprehensive study of the impact of West Indian cricket on those of Caribbean birth and descent in Britain. The book traces the history of the relationship between West Indian cricket and the Caribbean diaspora from the beginning of mass immigration to Britain in the 1950s. It explores the links between Caribbean cricket, migration, identity and presence, and the recent challenges cricket has faced in Britain as a prime source of pride for the Caribbean diaspora.

The book reflects on how West Indian cricket evolved into providing a common focus for those from different Caribbean countries, social backgrounds and experiences. It combines historical and sociological perspectives with traces of humour and focuses on pivotal events and personalities.

The end result is a thoughtful and timely piece of work which should make a major contribution to the continuing debate about the impact of West Indian cricket, and appeal to cricket fans and non-cricket aficionados alike.

Lord Bill Morris of Handsworth OJ

Introduction

In 1948, a landmark event symbolised the beginning of large-scale post-war migration from the Caribbean to Britain. When the Empire Windrush ship sailed from Jamaica on 24 May, there were 492 passengers and six stowaways on board.[1] The passengers included more than 400 migrants from the Caribbean with aspirations to create a new future in Britain.

Two years after the arrival of the Windrush and the emergence of a small black Caribbean presence in Britain, the West Indies cricket team beat England for the first time on English soil at Lord's. This triumph was witnessed by the Trinidadian calypsonian, Lord Beginner, who also arrived in Britain on the Windrush. While celebrating victory, Lord Beginner was inspired to compose Victory Test Match which began with the memorable first line, Cricket Lovely Cricket.

For some Caribbean migrants who settled in Britain from the 1950s onwards, the performances of the West Indian cricket team symbolised progress and togetherness. West Indian victories against the England cricket team, and especially on English soil, provided West Indians resident in Britain with a source of pride and an opportunity to witness victory against representatives of the old colonial Empire.

The first colour television to arrive in our Guyanese/Barbadian family home in England was purchased to coincide with the 1973 West Indies tour. The television eventually arrived as the third test match began at Lord's. Therefore, we were able to invite our West Indian relatives and friends, Caribbean and British born, to congregate and view live coverage of the match. The common cause was to support West Indian cricket.

The cricket arena offered some migrants from the Caribbean, whether they were passionate cricket fans or not, with an opportunity to express a collective identity and experience a sense of camaraderie. The importance of West Indian cricket as a pan-Caribbean force was highlighted by Clive Lloyd during his tenure as the West Indies cricket team captain:

> As captain of the West Indies for ten years I can honestly say that cricket is the ethos around which West Indian society revolves. All our experiments in Caribbean integration either failed or have maintained a dubious survivability; but cricket remains the instrument of Caribbean cohesion – the remover of arid insularity and nationalistic prejudice. It is through cricket and its many spin-offs that we owe our Caribbean considerations and dignity abroad.[2]

Collectively, West Indian players appeared to accept the responsibilities of representing the hopes and aspirations of Caribbean migrants and their descendants in Britain. Months before the 2007 Cricket World Cup was held in the Caribbean, I attended an event organised at London Metropolitan University by the Barbados High Commission and the Barbados Tourism Authority. The event featured an update on preparations for the World Cup by Stephen Alleyne, Chief Executive Officer of the Barbados Local Organising Committee with contributions from Garry Sobers, Gordon Greenidge and Gladstone Small.

Alongside them on the panel was the former West Indian fast-bowler and team manager, Wes Hall, who toured England as a West Indian player during the 1960s/1970s. During his short talk, followed by a question and answer session, Wes Hall underlined the importance of the relationship between cricket and the Caribbean community in Britain. Hall recalled how he was often reminded by West Indians he met in Britain that if the West Indies team were defeated by England, they wouldn't go back to work the following morning. Taking a day off work was better than enduring the humiliation and ridicule from their English work colleagues.

According to Hilary Beckles, English players on the opposing team were thrown into a panic when they faced Viv Richards. They sensed that for the Antiguan batsman, cricket was the business of history and politics and the struggle against injustice and inequality.[3]

For Richards, competing against England was more than just a competitive game of international cricket. It was an opportunity to assert himself and his colleagues as a collective Caribbean force. In this way, cricket was viewed as one of the few arenas in which a black person from the Caribbean could compete with a white person on the basis of equality.

These motivational forces revealed a sense of muscularity that opposing England cricketers had not previously experienced. Derek Pringle, the former England bowler and now journalist, played against the West Indies in eleven test matches:

> When you bowled at Richards, you knew you were about to be assaulted and that it was indeed personal. If it was his day, and inevitably it was, humiliation, the worst thing for a sportsman, was virtually guaranteed.[4]

Viv Richards was more than willing to express an understanding of the West Indian migrant's social condition and daily struggles in England. As captain of the 1988 West Indies tour of England, Richards outlined the responsibility of representing the Caribbean community living in Britain. He considered that it was important for him to perform for West Indians in Britain 'who don't have too great a life', including those who worked on the London Underground train system.[5]

Several years after Richards stated that the aspirations of the British-resident Caribbean diaspora and the mood of regional Caribbean self-assertion were key motivational tools, the importance of West Indian cricket to the British-resident diaspora began to experience a decline. This decline appears to be irreversible as cricket struggles to penetrate the imagination of the British-born Caribbean community.

Has this trend been largely influenced by West Indian underachievement by the players on the pitch and poor administration and management by the West Indian Cricket Board (WICB)? Has a disconnect in the relationship between West Indian cricket and the Caribbean diaspora been shaped by changing patterns of West Indian self-identification and expression? How relevant is cricket now to the British Caribbean diaspora's psyche, social identity and sense of nationhood?

In this book, I reflect on events, beyond the boundary and on the field of play, which influenced the development of the social, cultural and political impact of cricket on British Caribbean communities from the arrival of the Empire Windrush onwards. I will also examine the interplay and relationship between West Indian cricket and Caribbean diaspora migration, presence and identity.

What are the factors which have increasingly challenged the importance of cricket as a cultural and social force, and as a marker of identity for current descendants of the Windrush generation? While assessing these factors, I will explore the changing patterns of transgenerational British Caribbean identity, which may no longer view West Indian cricket as a primary source of self-esteem.

Chapter 1

THE ORIGINS OF WEST INDIAN CRICKET

The arrival of the Empire Windrush, emerging Caribbean migration to Britain and cricket, lovely, cricket

The game of cricket in the British-ruled Caribbean emerged and began to develop in the early nineteenth century. For the ruling white colonial planter class, there was a continual desire to reinforce social and cultural barriers between themselves and the majority black African population. The introduction of cricket was a welcome additional pastime for the colonial elite and British army soldiers stationed in the Caribbean. Through its assumed associated high values as a social activity, cricket began to be utilised as an additional tool to culturally and socially distinguish the planter class from the rest of Caribbean colonial society.

Therefore, cricket was imported as an activity that the planter class utilised to establish their cultural superiority. According to Hilary Beckles, the white West Indian community in the Caribbean was a dependent one that 'looked towards the imperial centre as the source for all normative values and institutional edifices.'[1] For the ruling elite in the British-ruled Caribbean, the importation of cricket maintained identifiable cultural ties with the imperial centre of British colonial rule.

As Professor Clem Seecharan outlines, cricket in the Caribbean was reserved for the colonial ruling class and became an epitome of Englishness. The rest of the population was deliberately excluded, which served to encapsulate the virtues of what was perceived to be a higher form of civilisation. While the colonial elite played the game, blacks were usually required to undertake peripheral tasks. This included the preparation of the playing area, 'the weeding or scything of the ground, retrieving the ball from the ubiquitous cane field, and performing a range of chores connected with the entertainment of guests.'[2]

Towards the end of the nineteenth century, cricket developed into an activity that was taken up by all groups in Caribbean colonial society. The broad intention of the planter elite, merchants and colonial administrators was to administer and play the game as a superior cultural pursuit, and inculcate ideas of English high values and virtues to the rest of the population. As Brian Stoddart asserts, in Barbados, cricket became a civilising mechanism for this group, a source of reaffirmation of social standards for its players and a display of civilised behaviour for its spectators, especially those from a colonial Caribbean 'working class' background.[3]

Caribbean people from the perceived lower social orders and other main non-white ethnic groups, including the descendants of African slaves, mixed-race descendants of European and Africans and indentured labourers from India and China, continued to develop an interest in the evolving cricket culture. Participation increased throughout the cricket-playing English-speaking Caribbean and progressed across the visible economic, class and race divisions. The planter class, in a changing post-emancipation Caribbean society, struggled to push back this tide of enthusiasm. As Michael Manley outlines:

> Particularly after the emancipation of the slaves in 1838, the rest of the population began to emulate the habits and practices of the elite and even to create parallel, though less well endowed, institutions of their own.[4]

Cricket clubs were established to satisfy the need for the various social groups to play a team sport in a heavily stratified colonial society. These institutions established their own class distinctions and identities, and appealed to members who possessed their required racial and social characteristics.

In Beyond a Boundary, CLR James outlines how cricket clubs clearly represented the different social strata in Trinidad in the early twentieth century. At the top of the scale was the Queens Park club whose members were mainly white and wealthy; Shamrock was the club of the old Catholic families; Stingo members were black with no status; Maple was the club of the brown-skinned middle class and Shannon was the club of the Trinidadian black lower middle class.[5]

In 1857, Jamaicans established the St.Jago, the Vere and Clarendon cricket clubs, where membership was restricted to the propertied white classes. Both coloureds and blacks were excluded from membership.[6]

In British Guiana, members of the Georgetown Cricket Club were usually whites, Portuguese and those with light skin complexions. The Demerara Cricket Club represented Georgetown's black lower middle class population; East Indians played for the East Indian Cricket Club; and Chinese cricketers represented the Chinese Sports Club.[7]

As Hilary Beckles notes, the Wanderers Club in Barbados, which was established in 1877, had an exclusively white merchant elite and planter membership until the end of the nineteenth century.[8] Pickwick was the preserve of the white upper and middle class, while the Spartan Cricket Club existed to serve the propertied upper and middle Barbadian coloured class.[9]

By the first decade of the twentieth century, cricket continued its progress as a growing social and cultural force. All social groups played the game, with varying degrees of enthusiasm and seriousness, in hierarchical British-ruled colonial societies. However, strict social and cultural divisions continued to be enforced through the cricket club system as clubs were established in Barbados, British Guiana, Trinidad and Jamaica.

Cricket's rituals of fair play and codes of conduct had an inbuilt set of perceived superior social values. The colonial elite attempted to promote these patterns of behaviour as desirable English virtues to be absorbed by the rest of colonial society. The game provided an opportunity for social distances to be marginally reduced and a level of contact to exist through the avenue of competitive sport. This occurred between the various social groups, despite having barely existed outside the economic and social relationships of boss and worker or shopkeeper and customer.

Cricket also provided a social arena for the non-white Caribbean population to witness a level of achievement and celebrate sporting triumphs and heroes. In 1899, the Spartan Cricket Club, consisting of the upper and middle Barbadian coloured class, won the island's Challenge Cup by defeating teams with all-white members. Spartan's victory served to undermine the ideology of white supremacy in Caribbean cricket culture.[10]

Although club cricket within each Caribbean territory was on the increase towards the end of the nineteenth century, developing regular competitive cricket between individual territories, and a team representing a pan-Caribbean identity, was difficult to organise. This was mainly due to the inconvenience and logistics of travel from one territory to another, especially as this was years before the age of regular inter-island air travel.

The first competitive inter-colonial cricket match was played in 1865 when Barbados hosted British Guiana in Bridgetown. Despite its non-island geographical location on mainland South America, British

Guiana, re-named as Guyana after independence from British-rule in 1966, was historically, politically and culturally linked to the islands since British colonisation in the eighteenth century. As John Major outlines in his book which explores the social history of world cricket's early years, interest in this match in Barbados was so great that employers released their workers to attend play in the afternoon.[11]

As Michael Manley outlines, Jamaica was less actively involved than Barbados, British Guiana and Trinidad in early inter-colonial cricket matches. This was not because of any absence of enthusiasm or interest, but mainly due to Jamaica's geographical location in the Caribbean, which is about 1,000 miles away from the other three territories that were within a day's sail of each other by steamship.[12]

As cricket continued to develop in the region, a representative regional team was finally selected in 1886. The first West Indian team was an all-white side that, albeit, toured America and Canada with mixed fortunes in terms of results. From August to September 1886, the West Indies played thirteen matches in America and Canada. The team won six matches, lost five matches and two were drawn. [13] West Indian cricket would have to wait for more than forty years for their first significant cricket moment.

In 1928, the West Indies played their first official test match as part of a three-match test tour of England. Their squad for this tour was a mix of white and black players selected from the four major British Caribbean sugar territories: Barbados, British Guiana, Trinidad and Jamaica. To enforce the continuing system of white leadership, which reflected Caribbean colonial society divisions, the team captaincy was entrusted to a white and, largely, English school-educated Jamaican, Karl Nunes.

Thus, a pastime that had been imported by the colonial elite was transformed into a mass participation sport with class and race divisions firmly intact. Caribbean cricket now had an official regional representative cricket team; in the form of a collection of British-ruled territories that could compete with the 'mother country' on British soil.

The 1928 West Indian touring team was defeated in all three test matches, but it had established the first official federal Caribbean institution with an identifiable West Indian identity. The West Indies emerged as the only international cricket team which represented a regional collection of British colonial territories.

The West Indian player who enhanced his reputation during the 1928 tour, despite the three test match defeats, was the Trinidadian, Learie Constantine. His scoring rate during the test series was comparatively low compared to his performances in the other tour matches. However, including his efforts in the tour matches, Constantine scored 1381 runs in first class matches for an average of 34.50.[14] Learie Constantine's flamboyant talent with bat and ball embraced a visible Caribbean style of play rarely seen by English cricket spectators.

Constantine's performances helped to earn him a contract playing for Nelson in the Lancashire Cricket League, performing for spectators who were unfamiliar with the regular sight of a black person. After the 1928 tour, Constantine continued to consolidate his position as the first black West Indian sports star and a pioneering early Caribbean migrant in Britain.

During the 1928 tour, the West Indies played three test matches at Lord's and The Oval in London and at Old Trafford in Manchester. However, there is no evidence of a significant West Indian presence amongst the spectators attending these matches. This was twenty years before the beginning of significant levels of migration from the Caribbean to Britain, and there were no seeds of a relationship to develop between a British-resident Caribbean diaspora and West Indian cricket. This began to change with the arrival of the Windrush generation.

On 21 June 1948, a former British troopship called the Empire Windrush docked in Tilbury, Essex with more than 400 passengers from the Caribbean. The majority of the West Indian arrivals were Jamaican men intent on creating a new future for themselves in Britain. Moreover, the arrival of the Windrush heralded the beginning of mass migration to Britain from its Caribbean territories.

The writer, Onyekachi Wambu, who edited Empire Windrush: Fifty Years of Writing About Black Britain, describes the arrival of the Windrush as the first ship that 'brought home the people of Empire from their peripheral margins to the metropolitan centre itself.'[15] The Windrush was soon followed by two arrivals in Liverpool: October 1948, the Orbita brought 180 migrants and three months later, thirty-nine Jamaicans, fifteen of them women, arrived on the Reina del Pacifo.[16]

Some of the Caribbean immigrants were returning to Britain after serving there during the Second World War. For example, 13,500 workers from the Caribbean were recruited by the Royal Air Force (RAF) to work as ground crew and 1,000 technicians worked in the munitions factories in Liverpool.[17]

After ten years as a successful Caribbean professional import for Nelson in the Lancashire Cricket League, Learie Constantine became a Ministry of Labour Welfare Officer during the Second World War. His remit was to improve the opportunities and represent the interests of West Indians who had been recruited to join the war effort in Britain.

The 1948 Nationality Act granted British citizenship to those living in Britain's colonies. From 1948, slightly more than 5,000 Caribbean migrants arrived in Britain during the following five years.[18] As British passport holders, this allowed Caribbean migrants to work and live in Britain. Other migrants would soon follow as they sought an alternative to high levels of unemployment in the Caribbean and responded to the need for manpower to rebuild Britain. There was also the option of joining friends and family who could help them cope with the difficulties of migrant life in Britain. Some migrants were also motivated by a sense of adventure and self-improvement that could only be realised by leaving the Caribbean.

Caribbean migrants who arrived in Britain in the 1950s had a sense of personal identity and nationhood closely tied to their British-ruled colonial homeland, and self-perceptions of ethnicity and social class experience. Their assumptions of Britishness and the understanding of their historical and political connections to Britain were soon to be seriously challenged. However, these notions of identity on arrival in Britain were, arguably, stronger than being self-identifiable as 'West Indian.'

In Andrea Levy's novel, Small Island, a tale of Caribbean migration and personal and social relationships in wartime and post-war Britain, Gilbert Joseph leaves Jamaica and returns to Britain where he served in the RAF during the Second World War. A recalled wartime conversation experienced by Gilbert with a couple of African-American servicemen, illustrates the post-war migrant West Indian's mixed assumptions of nationhood and identity.

Gilbert (nicknamed Joe by the African-American servicemen) explains that he is British but not English, as he is from Jamaica, with Britain being his mother country. One of the American serviceman expresses a sense of confusion:

> 'Joe, I don't altogether understand what you're saying. Jamaica is in England and who is your mother?' Gilbert responds, 'No, Jamaica is not in England but it is part of the British Empire.' The American enquires, 'The British Empire, you say. And where would that be, Joe?' Gilbert concludes, 'There are plenty countries belong to the British Empire.' Gilbert, once again, attempts to conclude, 'Jamaica is a colony. Britain is our Mother Country. We are British but we live in Jamaica.'[19]

My Afro-Guyanese mother's migration stories often tell of meeting large numbers of West Indians, for the first time, from other Caribbean territories after arriving in Britain in the early 1960s. As she often remarks, 'I didn't meet a Jamaican until I came to England.' As Catherine Hall asserts, it was the post-war Caribbean migrants who became West Indian in Britain. By meeting people from other Caribbean territories for the first time, they recognised a common identity and the need to confront the racial realities of their new lives in Britain.[20]

The academic, writer and broadcaster, Stuart Hall, migrated to Britain from Jamaica in the 1950s. According to Hall, after limited interaction with other people from the Caribbean in Jamaica, he discovered a sense of pan-Caribbean self-identity soon after arriving in Britain:

> You know, I'd never seen another West Indian. I'd occasionally glimpsed the odd Barbadian – he was the strangest thing I ever saw. But when Karl Jackman came, incidentally, to teach me Latin in the sixth form (in Jamaica), and opened his mouth, I thought I'd never heard a sound like that. I discovered I was West Indian in London – that's where you discovered you were West Indian. [21]

The Trinidadian writer, Sam Selvon, arrived in England in 1950. His post-war migrant tale, The Lonely Londoners, focused on the experiences of a group of West Indian men surviving and reinventing themselves in 1950s London. Selvon also began interacting with other people from the Caribbean for the first time upon arrival in England:

> When I left Trinidad in 1950 and went to England, one of my first experiences was living in a hostel with people from Africa and India and all over the Caribbean. It is strange to think that I had to cross the Atlantic and be thousands of miles away, in a different culture and environment, for it to come about that, for the first time in my life, I was living among Barbadians and Jamaicans and others from my part of the world. If I had remained in Trinidad I might never have had the opportunity to be at such close quarters to observe and try to understand the differences and prejudices that exist from islander to islander.[22]

At the age of 13, Vince Reid was one of the migrants who travelled from Jamaica to Britain on the Windrush. Two years later, he joined the RAF. He described his identity and concept of nationhood as being rooted in the colonial relationship between Jamaica and Britain:

Jamaicans were always singing songs like 'Land of Hope and Glory and mother of the free' and 'Rule Britannia, Britannia rules the waves.' The training that we had was typically British. And we accepted that, on a whole. Wholeheartedly I feel that, speaking as how I felt myself at that time that we, as Jamaicans, were allies to Britain, whether we were miles or thousand miles away. And this comes to many of us joining the war effort. And this was a feeling to know that we were defending Britain. And, of course, we were compelled, in a way, to say, well, we want to defend Britain in certain respects.[23]

Cy Grant, who later experienced a degree of success as an actor and entertainer on stage, film and British television, arrived in Britain from British Guiana during the Second World War to join the RAF. Although influenced by the relationship between British Guiana and British colonial rule, Grant suggested that his ethnicity, described as a coloured person in British Guiana then as a black person after settling in Britain, was a core feature of his identity. Grant's identity eventually shifted to being a black Caribbean migrant in Britain, but he didn't experience a sense of being racially demoted:

> We definitely had privileges (living in British Guiana) over the people of purely black descent. It's only when I came to England that I realised, fortunately, that I was, in fact, black. And people referred to me as black, you know. It seemed strange when I came to England.[24]

With these variations on identity, which were not essentially pan-Caribbean, large numbers of black Caribbean migrants to Britain in the 1950s brought their cricket culture with them. This was an act of appreciation for a game that had evolved into a site of Caribbean aspirations through success on the field of play, and was closely associated with colonial Caribbean society, class and race. VS Naipaul observed this in reference to the direct relationship between cricket and the population in his native Trinidad:

> Cricket has always been more than a game in Trinidad. In a society which demanded no skills and offered no rewards to merit, cricket was the only activity which permitted a man to grow to his full stature and to be measured against international standards. Alone on a field, beyond obscuring intrigue, the cricketer's true worth could be seen by all. His race, education, wealth did not matter. We had no scientists, engineers, explorers, soldiers or poets. The cricketer was our only hero figure.[25]

Two years after the arrival of the Windrush, a historic West Indian cricket success in England was celebrated amongst the small Caribbean migrant population in Britain and throughout the Caribbean. In June 1950, after losing the first test match at Old Trafford, Manchester, the West Indies beat England in the second test match at Lord's by an impressive margin of 326 runs. The West Indies also triumphed in the remaining two matches at Trent Bridge, Nottingham and The Oval to secure a 3-1 series victory.

The West Indies won their first test series in 1934/1935 by beating England 2-1 in the Caribbean. However, this was the first time the West Indies had beaten England on English soil in a test match. The event unfolded at the spiritual headquarters of English cricket, which was also the base for world cricket's governing body, the Imperial Cricket Conference. According to Michael Manley, who was a student in London and later Prime Minister of Jamaica, the West Indies victory at Lord's was clearly symbolic:

> The victory was more than just a sporting success. It was the proof that a people was coming of age. They had bested the masters at their own game on their home turf. They had done so with good nature, with style, often with humour, but with conclusive effectiveness. Rae, Stollmeyer, Worrell, Weekes and Walcott had made hundreds of runs to the delight of thousands and to establish the foundations upon which victory was to rest. The victory itself was procured by 'those little pals of mine, Ramadhin and Valentine.'[26]

At Lord's, the combined bowling performances of Sonny Ramadhin and Alf Valentine, a vibrant symbol of young Indo-Caribbean and Afro-Caribbean collaborative effort, captured a total of eighteen wickets. 'The three Ws' black, Barbadian, middle-order batting force of Everton Weekes, Frank Worrell and Clyde Walcott also made notable contributions in this match and throughout the series. Their prolific displays in England helped to erase the Caribbean colonial belief that batting was a craft that white batsmen were better disposed to. Batting was perceived more as an art form as opposed to the muscular activity of fast bowling, a responsibility traditionally undertaken in the West Indies by black cricketers.

Clyde Walcott contributed to the West Indian victory at Lord's by scoring a memorable 168 in the second innings. Walcott, along with his West Indian team colleagues, was elated with joy at the end of the game. Realising that they had created cricket history, he described the West Indian players as being 'intoxicated with delight and pleasure'[27] as they made their way back to their dressing room. Speaking on a BBC

World Service radio programme which explored the enduring legacy of the Lord's victory, Clyde Walcott explained how much the result at Lord's meant to the Caribbean people he knew in Britain:

> In those days, coloured people or black people, whatever you want to call them, were more or less given a hard time. And they said how, and this was after the test, proud they felt to go into work or to school, the next day or the Monday or whenever it was, having beaten England.[28]

The 1950 Lord's victory provided Caribbean migrants in Britain, including the small group of West Indian supporters at Lord's, with a definitive symbol of West Indian arrival and an early opportunity to express a collective migrant identity. Sam King from Jamaica, who returned to Britain on the Windrush after serving there in the RAF, refers to the 1950 West Indies victory at Lord's as a significant moment. According to Sam King, the events at Lord's instantly raised the profile of Caribbean migrants and created a path for incorporation and assimilation into wider British society:

> (Now) after that, the British people, realising that the minority people from the colonies here had beaten them at cricket, we were not as stupid as a lot of them assumed or wanted us to be stupid. And, even in the factories, gradually, it starts permeating, that if you teach these people machinery, they will be good machinists. And in the forties, a few of us were engineers or whatever it is, and then they realise, if you give them the opportunity, they will be good non-commissioned officers, and if they had the education, they'll be officers. Yes, it was a milestone for the people from the colonies.[29]

For Baroness Ros Howells, who migrated to Britain from Grenada in the early 1950s, the victory at Lord's was the moment when elements of West Indian cricket and music culture arrived in Britain at the same time:

> Don't forget 1950, that's the year we won the test at Lord's. Ramadhin and Valentine and the calypso. I think that changed the whole face of cricket. It was no longer the quiet game where you sat on the terraces and gently clapped when somebody scored. Caribbean people took over and we brought the steel band, we brought the calypso.[30]

Although Baroness Howells' claim that 'Caribbean people took over' could be interpreted as an exaggeration, the small but vocal West Indian support at Lord's made a notable impact. The calypso referred to by Baroness Howells arrived at Lord's following the confirmation of West Indian victory.

The West Indian supporters were amongst the aggregate estimated attendance of 112,000 spectators across the five days of play.[31] As Stuart Hall points out, some West Indians in the crowd made their presence felt by 'exuberant shouting, singing and the rattling of tin cans throughout the game in ways that astonished the natives and transformed for ever the ethos of test cricket.'[32] A report in The Times newspaper commented on the joy expressed by West Indian spectators at the end of the match:

> That was the end, suitably acclaimed by a rush of West Indian supporters, one armed with an instrument of the guitar family. Lord's will be a dull place indeed without these West Indian followers, who maintained a loud commentary on every ball bowled during the match, and who, when it was over, were singing with delight which rightfully belonged to them.[33]

A minority of the West Indian support at Lord's had been resident in England before the beginning of post-second world war mass migration to Britain. Allan Rae, the Jamaican batsman, recalls in Vijay P. Kumar's comprehensive study of the 1950 West Indies tour of England, how he received a message from a man in the West Indian team's hotel foyer who wanted to meet the Jamaican players after the match. The overjoyed man, who identified himself as Leon, had been living in England since 1900 and with tears in his eyes quoted from the Bible, 'Let now they humble servant depart in peace for my eyes have seen it all.' He then gave some gifts to the Jamaican players before departing.[34]

Amongst the West Indian contingent in the crowd who had arrived on The Windrush were the Trinidadian calypsonians, Egbert 'Lord Beginner' Moore and Aldwyn 'Lord Kitchener' Roberts. At the end of the match, Kitchener prepared to lead some West Indian supporters around the ground and then through Central London on a spontaneous victory parade.

This was an exuberant public display of Caribbean collectiveness that had not been seen before in Britain. Lord Beginner, with encouragement from other jubilant West Indian migrants, honoured the occasion by composing the Victory Test Match calypso song, which began with the memorable first line, Cricket Lovely Cricket:

> Cricket lovely Cricket,
> At Lord's where I saw it;
> Cricket lovely Cricket,

At Lord's where I saw it;
Yardley tried his best
But Goddard won the Test.
They gave the crowd plenty fun;
Second Test and West Indies won.
With those two little pals of mine
Ramadhin and Valentine.

The King was there well attired,
So they started with Rae and Stollmeyer;
Stolly was hitting balls around the boundary;
But Wardle stopped him at twenty.
Rae had confidence,
So he put up a strong defence;
He saw the King was waiting to see,
So he gave him a century.
With those two little pals of mine
Ramadhin and Valentine.

This triumph may have been considered by some Caribbean migrants in Britain to be a pan-Caribbean success story. However, the majority of the 1950 West Indies squad of sixteen players came from three of the traditional 'big four' British colonial territories of Barbados, Trinidad and Jamaica. Robert Christiani was the only player selected from British Guiana. Sonny Ramadhin made history during the 1950 series by being the first Indo-Caribbean cricketer to represent the West Indies in a test match. In just over twenty years on from the 1950 series, Rohan Kanhai would become the first Indo-Caribbean captain of the West Indies cricket team.

Although Lord Beginner doesn't highlight the ethnicity of individual team members, the players acclaimed by him in the first two verses of the calypso represented various strands of Caribbean ethnicity, identity and nationhood. An Indian and white Trinidadian, Sonny Ramadhin and Jeff Stollmeyer, a black and mixed heritage Jamaican, Alf Valentine and Allan Rae, were captained at Lord's by a white Barbadian, John Goddard. Beginner recognised the important contributions made by all five of these players. Ramadhin and Valentine, 'those little pals of mine', received special praise for their bowling achievements. Lord Beginner also reminds us that this collective West Indian success over the colonial power was witnessed by the reigning British monarch, King George VI.

The numbers of migrants from the Caribbean continued to increase throughout the decade following the victory at Lord's: From 1953 to

1958, 125,000 people migrated to the Caribbean from Britain.[35] When the West Indies team arrived in 1957 for a five-match test tour of England, they received an enthusiastic reception from a vocal group of British-resident West Indians. An article in the Daily Telegraph newspaper commented on the connection between rising levels of migration from the Caribbean to Britain, the 1957 West Indian team's arrival in Britain, and the growing relationship between the team and West Indians resident in Britain:

> The eighth West Indies cricket team to tour England arrived yesterday under skies which were a respectable imitation of their own blue and to a boisterous and colourful reception. Since John Goddard brought his last team here seven years ago, their supporters have multiplied many times. Yesterday the calypsos began at Southampton in the morning, continued from a demonstrative crowd of 300 at Waterloo in the afternoon, and was still going strong in the evening outside the Kensington hotel in which Goddard held his Press conference.[36]

A further 113,000 migrants arrived from the Caribbean between 1958 and the end of 1961.[37] After this, the 1962 Commonwealth Immigration Act introduced a system of employment vouchers that limited the migrant intake, and there was a rush to enter Britain before this legislation effectively closed the doors to Caribbean migrants.[38]

Reports were often relayed back to the Caribbean from Britain that, despite the hardships and challenges, there was an opportunity to gain employment and join family members and friends who had managed to survive and settle. For some migrants, the motivation was to work and earn enough money to send back to their families, or to save money to return to the Caribbean with after a temporary stay in Britain. These were also significant motivational tools for Caribbean people from the lower end of the socio-economic scale. For these migrants, opportunities back home in the Caribbean were often limited and had worsened during the period immediately after the end of the Second World War.

For some Caribbean migrants in Britain, the daily grind of migrant life was often a series of hardships, challenges and discrimination from mainstream British society. There was also the prospect of open hostility and violent attacks. Street conflicts and confrontations in the metropolitan areas where Caribbean migrants lived were not uncommon.

In 1958, in Nottingham and Notting Hill, London, increased levels of racial hostility were accompanied by violence and brawls between some members of the Caribbean community and white gangs. The following year in Notting Hill, Kelso Cochrane, an Antiguan, was killed after an assault by a group of white youths. The painful experiences of hostility, voluntary exile and social isolation in Britain are clearly expressed by the Trinidadian migrant, Moses Aloetta, in Sam Selvon's book, The Lonely Londoners:

> Looking at things in general life really hard for the boys in London. This is a lonely city, if it was that we didn't get together now and then to talk about things back home, we would suffer like hell. Here is not like home where you have friends all about. In the beginning you would think that is a good thing, that nobody minding your business, but after a while you want to get in company, you want to go to somebody house and eat a meal, you want to go on excursion to the sea, you want to go and play football and cricket.[39]

Associating and indulging in social activities provided a temporary respite to the common anxieties of migration and feelings of disillusionment. The self-belief that could be drawn from West Indian cricket could not erase the dispiriting aspects of migrant life, but it offered some Caribbean migrants the continued opportunity to develop a relationship with West Indian cricket as a marker of identity.

The academic, broadcaster and writer, Mike Phillips, was born in Guyana and arrived in Britain as a twelve year old boy in 1956. With his brother, Trevor, he wrote the book, Windrush, The Irresistible Rise of Multi-Racial Britain. As Mike Phillips suggests, cricket, and West Indian cricket in particular, provided some Caribbean migrants with their primary source of expression. It gave them the confidence to assert themselves and chartered a path to recognition and assimilation:

> There was only one way of expressing West Indian character and a Caribbean presence, and that was cricket. Because it came out of Britain in the first place it offered a sort of bridge into the English culture. We understood what it meant to be part of this society, partly because we understood cricket. The English perceived cricket as a sort of commentary on themselves and who they were. We had a very similar sense of who we were coming out of the nature of cricket and the way it was played. To be here (in Britain) and be exposed to cricket matches between the West Indies and English was, in fact, to be a home from home.

It was the one thing that wasn't strange or alien to us and, I suspect, the one thing about us that was not strange and alien to the English. We could assert ourselves in a way that we couldn't do in any other way. The sheer beauty, elegance, force and aggressiveness from batsmen like the three Ws (Everton Weekes, Frank Worrell and Clyde Walcott), in the sense in which they were standing up for themselves, was unique and very important to us at the time living in Britain.[40]

In the British feature film, Wondrous Oblivion, released in 2003, a Jamaican migrant family headed by Dennis Samuels move into a house in 1960s Britain. They become the first black family to reside in a South London neighbourhood. According to the film's writer and director, Paul Morrison, a Londoner of Jewish descent, the experience of isolation as a Caribbean migrant family was shared with the Wondrous Oblivion production team by a family living near one of the film's location points:

> South London was too noisy and too difficult to film in, so we filmed in St.Albans. There was just one Afro-Caribbean family living in the street in St.Albans where we filmed and they, very much, befriended us and understood what we were doing, and shared the experience of arriving in Britain and being the only black family on the street.[41]

Dennis Samuels was played by the actor, Delroy Lindo, a British-born American of Jamaican parentage. Lindo made it a condition of his participation in Wondrous Oblivion that Morrison understood 'the depth of the hurt that apparently small acts of indifference or omission could cause in an individual and their family.'[42]

Dennis' close friend, Mr Johnson, was played by the actor, Louis Mahoney. Originally from Gambia, Mahoney represented Gambia at cricket in inter-colonial contests against Sierra Leone at the age of seventeen. He arrived in Britain during the 1960s and continued playing cricket for various club sides including the Ilford cricket club in Essex. As a West African migrant in London, Mahoney viewed West Indian victories against England as a source of upliftment in a climate of racism and discrimination in 1960s Britain.

When I spoke to Louis Mahoney he fondly remembered watching West Indies play England in the 1960s and 1970s, witnessing Colin Cowdery walk out to bat with a broken arm to save the game for England at Lord's against the West Indies in 1963, and drinking in London pubs with the Australian fast bowler, Dennis Lillie, who he described as 'having an eye for the ladies.'[43]

Days after settling in his new South London home, Dennis Samuels, with the help of Louis Mahoney's character, Mr Johnson, begins to carefully roll the lawn in his small back garden. Dennis then proceeds to construct a cricket practice area in his garden complete with fully covered netting. He helps to coach his daughter and their young, cricket-besotted, Jewish schoolboy neighbour in the art of batting, bowling and fielding and refers to his 'bible' as CLR James', Beyond the Boundary.

Subsequently, Dennis' home and back garden are badly damaged in a racist arson attack. Some sympathetic members of the local community respond to this incident and help him construct a new netted cricket practice area. In this way, Dennis' marked out territory and symbol of arrival and identity is rebuilt.

For some Caribbean migrants to Britain, the social and cultural relationship with West Indian cricket was worn as a badge of identity and expressed a sense of togetherness in, often, hostile surroundings. The relationship between some of the British-resident diaspora and West Indian cricket, viewed as a pan-Caribbean institution, continued to develop throughout the 1950s/1960s.

Inter-territory antagonism and distrust failed to fragment West Indian cricket as a federal institution which, in turn, fed into elements of pan-Caribbean migrant self-awareness. However, political and economic tensions between individual West Indian territories made attempts to create federal self-government in the Caribbean relatively short-lived.

The West Indian Federation was created in 1958 as the political foundation for a federal West Indian nation, which would be self-governing and independent from British colonial rule. Yet by 1962, the unwillingness of the two largest island territories, Jamaica and Trinidad, to pursue the federal route led to the federation's eventual collapse. Once the concept of pan-Caribbean political federalism had disintegrated, Jamaica and Trinidad emerged as independent nation states.

As the West Indian Federation fell apart, an alternative symbol of Caribbean regional togetherness, leadership and self-rule began to emerge. The WICB finally overcame their reluctance to appoint a full-time black captain for the West Indies cricket team when Frank Worrell was appointed captain for the 1960/1961 tour of Australia. The Jamaican, George Headley, had been given the captaincy for just one test match in 1948. However, Worrell was the first black player appointed for an entire test series and his appointment marked the end of an era of unbroken white West Indian cricket captaincy.

As Tony Cozier, the Barbadian cricket commentator and writer, points out, white captaincy had been a consistent feature of West Indian cricket, and reflected colonial Caribbean society's general distrust of black self-rule:

> Up until the 1950s the chief of police in most territories was white; the headmasters of the best schools were white. The priests were white. And so cricket simply reflected society. Later on, with the advances of the independence movement, cricket played its part – because the game had such an important place in the psyche of the people. They agitated for Worrell to become captain and they wanted the teams in the territories to be led by the outstanding black players: Clyde Walcott in British Guiana, Everton Weekes in Barbados.[44]

When Frank Worrell appeared for the first test match in Brisbane, which finished in a dramatic tie, he became a black Caribbean captain playing under the newly established, but soon to be extinct, West Indian flag of federation. The West Indian team's organising board, the WICB, continued as a long established Caribbean regional institution. As Michael Manley observed, in reference to Frank Worrell's return from the test series in Australia:

> In the meantime, many of the politicians of the West Indies had drawn no discernible inspiration from the success of Worrell's side in Australia. The West Indian team was barely safe home when the newly formed Federation of the West Indies began to come unstuck.[45]

According to CLR James, who vigorously campaigned in Trinidad for Frank Worrell to be appointed as captain, the West Indian team's enthralling performances, Worrell's stature and leadership credentials, and a sense of arrival of Caribbean unity were the significant highlights of the tour. It was this combination of factors which resulted in such a huge farewell from the Australian public:

> I caught a glimpse of what brought a quarter of a million inhabitants of Melbourne into the streets to tell the West Indian cricketers goodbye, a gesture spontaneous and in cricket without precedent, one people speaking to another. Clearing their way with bat and ball, West Indians at that moment had made a public entry into the comity of nations.[46]

Those from the Caribbean diaspora in Britain who followed these developments with keen interest, could now point to an inspirational phase of political change within West Indian cricket. It was a development which offered a collective sense of social and political fulfilment, whether or not they were absolutely committed to the idea of pan-Caribbean political and economic federalism.

The flamboyant West Indian brand of aggressive and attractive cricket, which contributed to a thrilling series of rich entertainment in Australia, was openly appreciated by the vast majority of Australian spectators. However, if the West Indies had convincingly won the series, the farewell given to the West Indian players would, probably, not have attracted as many enthusiastic people on the streets of Melbourne.

On receiving reports of the entertaining cricket played during the West Indies 1960/1961 tour of Australia, the Marylebone Cricket Club (MCC) at Lord's recognised the financial rewards of altering their schedules and invited West Indian teams to tour England more frequently.[47] Between the 1950 series in England and Worrell's 1960/1961 Australian tour, the West Indies toured just once in England: a five match series in 1957, which they lost 3-0.

Following the 1960/1961 Australian tour, and up to and including 1973, the West Indies played four test series in England: in 1963, 1966, 1969 and 1973. During this period they won three series and lost only one, playing a total of sixteen matches against England in six different venues.[48] The quick succession of these tours offered West Indians in Britain more opportunities to congregate, attend matches and generate a closer relationship with the West Indies cricket team.

After the 1962 Commonwealth Immigration Act, the migration figures for Caribbean migrants decreased due to the restrictions of the voucher system. However, dependants of those slowly putting down more permanent roots in Britain could settle without vouchers. Between 1962 and 1967, 55,310 dependants of settled Caribbean migrants arrived in Britain.[49]

According to the 1966 UK census, an estimated 454,100 black West Indians were resident in Britain.[50] These figures also included children born in Britain to Caribbean parents. Their growing self-awareness of being second generation British-born West Indians in Britain, and sharing similar social, cultural and economic experiences with their parents, contributed to some of them also developing a relationship with West Indian cricket.

By the start of the 1963 series in England, the West Indies could now count on an increase in support since their last tour in 1957. As the Caribbean presence in Britain became more substantial, the significant Caribbean spectator presence at West Indies cricket matches in England became a more common sight. Ian Wooldridge, a journalist and author who documented the 1963 West Indies tour of England, commented in rather appreciative tones about the West Indian spectators at Lord's. In Wooldridge's opinion, 13 years after the historic 1950 test match, 'Lord's was alive again with cricket, lovely, cricket'[51] during the second test match:

> It seemed that half the West Indian population of London was crammed into the two tiers of seats at the Nursery End. They chattered, they laughed, they rose like passionate hot-gospellers to exhort one another to still noisier support. Their gaiety was contagious: it spread down to the wings of the wonderful old ground and met up again among the waistcoats and gold and scarlet ties beneath the Long Room windows. It also, for the first time on the tour, reached out to the middle to thaw out their long-frozen batsmen.[52]

After winning the final match of the 1963 tour at The Oval and, therefore, clinching the series 3-1, the emotional relationship between West Indians in Britain and the West Indian team was evident. The West Indies victory was accompanied by a raucous, but celebratory, pitch invasion by a large number of West Indian supporters. After being knocked over and submerged by the invading swarm, the Barbadian batsman, Conrad Hunte, described the increasing bond between the West Indian cricket team and the British-resident Caribbean community:

> I lay there on the ground terrified at being trampled upon as I looked up into the jubilant and excited faces of my compatriots. I need not have feared for my life or for my bat. Some West Indians got hold of my feet as I kicked and struggled to be free, others got hold of my arms and shoulders, some supported my waist and back, and carried me shoulder-high through a clear path in the crowd to the pavilion steps. There they carefully put me down and said, Now go in! I was safe indeed.[53]

The relationship between cricket and the Caribbean diaspora developed further as West Indian cricket clubs grew as centres of community, identity and spaces for social gatherings, and established themselves to participate in locally based competitive leagues and play against other Caribbean clubs and organisations.

One of the first established Caribbean cricket clubs in Britain was the Leeds Caribbean Cricket Club, which was formed in 1948 as a site for community gatherings and sporting activities for the emerging Caribbean community in Leeds. Harwood Williams, the club's Chairman, who was born in St.Kitts, explains how the club initially functioned as a transit point for early Caribbean migrants to Leeds and the West Yorkshire area:

> In the 50s and into the 60s, when the guys came here from the Caribbean, the club was used as a kind of base. Word would get round and someone from the person's family here in the UK would get in touch with the club. A person from that family would then meet and greet the person coming here at the club and find a place for them. The club was a home away from home and a place where you could share knowledge of where the jobs were and how to get accommodation in the area.[54]

As the club has developed, its social role has expanded into organised sports trips to the Caribbean, including St.Kitts, and playing cricket, football and netball against local teams. These trips have offered some members of the club, originally from St.Kitts, an organised opportunity to return for the first time to the island they migrated from in the 1960s and 1970s to live in Britain.

Earle Robinson, a cultural archivist and Leicester Caribbean Cricket Club trustee, took me on the short car trip to the Leicester club's ground, minutes away from Leicester's city centre. Earle, now in his 70s, migrated to Britain from Jamaica in 1958, arrived in Leicester and stayed there. As I chatted to Earle, the sounds of Johnny Nash drifted out of his car's music system. I was instantly transported back to my family's living-room in our flat in 1970s Britain where, on Sunday mornings, the music from Johnny Nash, Brooke Benton, Al Green and Sam Cooke was routine Sunday morning listening.

The Leicester Caribbean Cricket Club was formed in 1957 and set up by four men who had been members of the RAF, including two members from Antigua, one from Jamaica, and one from Guyana. As well as supporting cricket teams, the club has continued to develop into a social centre. Some of the older members of the West Indian community who once played cricket for the club, now regularly use the club's facilities to socialise with each other. The Leicester Caribbean Cricket Club is also connected to other Caribbean organisations in the area including Leicester's African Caribbean centre.

Gary Younge, a British-born journalist and author of Barbadian descent, was named after the Barbadian cricketer, Garry Sobers. The slight difference being that Gary Younge's first name contains one r instead of two. His parents migrated to Britain from Barbados and the family eventually settled in Stevenage, Hertfordshire. As Younge recalls:

> My parents were teenage sweethearts who arrived separately in London from Barbados in the early sixties, at the tail end of post-war migration. Britain sent for labour, but people arrived. They came to work and ended up living.[55]

Gary Younge also acknowledges the role the West Indian cricket club played as a community focal point in his home town of Stevenage:

> The black community's social life revolved around our cricket team, the Stevenage West Indians Sports and Social Club, or SWISSC. Both my father and my eldest brother used to play for SWISSC, and I used to score for them. About twice a year SWISSC would have a big party where each person would bring a dish (because there were no Caribbean caterers in the area), and a DJ who understood black music, generally from another town or someone's friend from London, would play calypso and reggae until the early morning.[56]

The mood of the diaspora, as arrivals from individual Caribbean territories emerged collectively as West Indians, continued to be influenced by their response to events associated with West Indies cricket. The West Indian cricket team and Caribbean cricket culture established itself as a marker of dignity, identity and black success for some Caribbean migrants attempting to settle and assert themselves in Britain. In a society where they were often viewed with indifference, suspicion and, at worst, extreme hostility, West Indian cricket continued to be a source of increased self-esteem and togetherness throughout the 1950s, 1960s and 1970s.

Whether they were cricket enthusiasts or not, West Indian victories over England offered some Caribbean migrants and their British-born descendants a communal point of reference where they could assume temporary superiority over their British work colleagues, friends and enemies. Rodney Hinds, born in Britain of Barbadian parents, is the sports editor of The Voice newspaper, a weekly publication aimed at Britain's Afro-Caribbean and African communities. Hinds points to witnessing his father's response to West Indian cricket success as the prime influence which shaped his eventual career path towards sports journalism:

> Growing up as a youngster in Britain in the 60s and 70s, my earliest sporting images were of black men doing very, very well at cricket and beating all comers. I know that looking at my father

when he was going to work at his factory, he would go, invariably, with his chest puffed out and immensely proud that his team, the West Indies, had essentially, beaten England and Australia, and beaten all comers. I recognised that at a very early age and, I think to some degree, that these formative years for me are about why I do what I do now as sports editor of the Voice newspaper. I saw sport as very important as whole. Football is king at the moment and will continue to be because of the vast sums of money and the profile it gets, but the starting point for me was cricket.[57]

Some of the first and emerging second generation British-resident Caribbean diaspora, despite the persistent reality of inter-island and generational differences, had begun to forge a collective relationship based on a shared interest in, and identity with, West Indian cricket.

'Those little pals of mine'. West Indian spin bowlers, Sonny Ramadhin (left) and Alf Valentine (right), during their tour of England, April 1950.
(Photo by Jimmy Sime/Getty Images)

Policeman, Colin Hutton, attempts to retrieve his helmet from a West Indian spectator at the West Indies v Australia World Cup group match at The Oval, 14th June 1975

Viv Richards drives during his 232, England v West Indies, 1st Test, Trent Bridge, June 1976. *(Photo by Patrick Eagar/Patrick Eagar Collection via Getty Images)*

Michael Holding leaves the field with Clive Lloyd and surrounded by spectators after taking 8 for 92 against England at the Oval, 16th August 1976.
(Photo by Keystone/Hulton Archive/Getty Images)

The Man Ezeke. Writer and performer of the song 'Who's Grovelling Now?'

'Who's Grovelling Now?' A record which became the unofficial anthem of West Indian supporters in Britain during the 1976 West Indies tour of England.

Alvin Kallicharan and his son, Rohan, at The Oval. A day before the 5th
England v West Indies test match in the 1980 series

**West Indian fans celebrate with a 'Blackwash' banner after their team wins
the 5th and final test match against England at The Oval in the 1984 series.**
(Adrian Murrell/Allsport)

Gordon Greenidge signs autographs for West Indian supporters after a pre - 2007 World Cup event held at London Metropolitan University on 1 November 2006 by the Barbados High Commission and the Barbados Tourism Authority.

The Caribbean Steel Band international perform during the lunch interval at Lord's, 6th May 2009. The first test match of the 2009 West Indies tour of England.

Ramnaresh Sarwan with Leicester Cricket Club Secretary, Krista Walters, at a reception held for the 2009 West Indies tour to England at the Leicester African Caribbean Centre.

Spectators at the Leeds Caribbean Cricket Club during a Twenty20 tournament in 2011. The Leeds club was one of the first Caribbean cricket clubs to be established in Britain.

Chapter 2

THE RISE OF WEST INDIAN CRICKET

An England captain is made to grovel, cricket's link to diaspora self-esteem and the emergence of the Caribbean-born English cricketer

My earliest cricket memories are located in one year, 1973. As a nine-year-old school boy of Caribbean descent living in England, I can still recall John Arlott's observant and humorous cricket commentary, and his gift for descriptive language delivered in a distinctive Hampshire burr. Arlott commentated on the Sunday John Player League limited-overs matches between English county teams which were regularly transmitted live on BBC television. Following the latest escapades of Barnaby the Bear, the animated antics of The Jackson Five and the adventures of Catweazle, John Player League cricket became an essential part of my Sunday television routine.

I briefly supported Sussex in the major county cricket competitions. This was because I felt sorry for them after they were defeated by Gloucestershire in the 1973 Gillette Cup final at Lord's. Alongside the FA Cup final at Wembley Stadium, the Gillette Cup final was the other annual major sporting occasion which I eagerly anticipated watching on television.

However, when it came to watching international cricket, it never occurred to me to support the England cricket team. I supported West Indian cricket because I felt my personal and cultural identity was intimately tied to the Caribbean. I was presented with an opportunity to support a group of players who came from the countries my family came from. As a metaphor for Caribbean representation in Britain, cricket was an activity that 'we' (as West Indians living in Britain) had a strong tradition in and could beat England at.

During summer months spent with family in the Caribbean, I would spend most days playing cricket with assorted relatives, friends and friends of friends. I was keen to prove that I was good enough to hold my own during any beach, street or yard cricket session. I refused to give up my wicket easily and, therefore, batted defensively. Although I was a committed West Indian fan, I admired the technique and dedication to occupying the crease adopted by Yorkshire and England's Geoffrey Boycott. In Barbados I was accused of 'batting like an Englishman'. This was something that I was strangely proud of.

Living in England, I played out West Indies verses England test matches with my friend, Nick, and West Indies verses Pakistan test matches with my friend, Shakil, in various backyards, public parks and streets. By regularly hitting Nick's bowling into his neighbour's garden and by clean bowling Shakil in our local park, I felt I was holding up a sense of West Indian honour against England and Pakistan.

Clive Lloyd had attended the same secondary school as my mother in Georgetown, Guyana; Rohan Kanhai and Alvin Kallicharan were from Port Mourant, Berbice, Guyana. Lengthy debates about West Indies cricket were always a key element of conversation when Caribbean men gathered during social occasions in our flat.

From the politics of cricket to politics and cricket, these cricket debates seamlessly blended in with robust reflections on political and social developments 'back home' in the Caribbean. Inevitably, for some of the Guyanese amongst the group, there was often heated analysis of the political battles between Forbes Burnham and Cheddi Jagan, and the continuing cycle of social and ethnic polarisation in Guyana.

The first television to arrive in our Guyanese/Barbadian household in London was purchased to coincide with the 1973 West Indies tour in England. On day three of the third and final test match at Lord's, we were also able to share the spectacle and tension of a bomb scare. In response to the PA announcer's request to evacuate the ground, hundreds of spectators decided, instead, to move across the boundary ropes and congregate on the grass while the police searched the stands.

Dickie Bird, the mildly eccentric English umpire, opted to wait it out by perching in the middle of the ground on the pitch-covers, surrounded by spectators. According to Bird, the substantial number of West Indian fans who surrounded his temporary perch, largely, seemed unperturbed by the unique emergency situation which had interrupted play at Lord's:

> The West Indian supporters did not seem in the least bit concerned. 'Don't you worry about the bomb, Mr Dickie Bird', they said to me. 'Just look at that total on the scoreboard and worry about that'. I glanced across: West Indies 652 for 8.[1]

In our living room, as well as the bomb scare at Lord's, the cricket drama on the field of play also provided a century each from Garry Sobers from Barbados, and Rohan Kanhai from Guyana, live in magnificent colour.

During this test series, the small living room in our housing association flat was typically full of Guyanese, Barbadian and Jamaican immigrants and their descendants sharing the experience of appreciating cricket in a distinctively Caribbean way. There was the communal desire to defeat a defined enemy, 'the English', the consumption of considerable quantities of rum, the sharing of traditional Caribbean food and snacks, and lengthy debates about the playing qualities of various West Indian players.

Most of the men exchanged tales of personal cricketing achievements in the Caribbean which were often exaggerated for dramatic effect. One of my uncles from Barbados, now resident in Canada, still proudly recalls how he bowled at a ferocious pace as a schoolboy in field cricket games in Barbados. As a result he earned the life-long nickname Tyson, after Frank 'Typhoon' Tyson, a fast bowler who represented England during the 1950s.

Regional Caribbean tensions, often laced with acerbic humour, occasionally rose to the surface. However, these disputes were inevitably drowned out with yelps of appreciation when a stylish West Indian batting stroke resulted in a boundary, or when an English batsman received a fierce short-pitched delivery from a West Indian fast bowler. The association with West Indian cricket acted as a Caribbean diaspora bonding agent. There was a sense of unity in exile.

For the black Caribbean diaspora during the 1970s, declaring an affiliation with the England national football team had limited appeal. There were very few pull factors. While some black Caribbean football fans supported English football clubs, and a minority attended domestic fixtures, this level of support rarely reached a sense of identification with the England team.

There were also no opportunities to gain inspiration by watching black players of Caribbean descent play for England. The first notable opportunity to arrive during this period was through Nottingham Forest's Viv Anderson. In 1978 at Wembley Stadium, with Czechoslovakia providing the opposition, Anderson became the first black footballer to represent England in a full international match. Anderson was an English-born player of Jamaican parentage who grew up supporting Brazil. As Anderson explains:

There weren't too many black players around at that time so I always followed the 1970's Brazil team, to see people who looked like myself playing the game. And what a side they were![2]

Cyrille Regis was born in French Guyana of St.Lucian and Guadeloupean parentage. He arrived in England at the age of five. In 1982, after making an impact as a player for West Bromwich Albion, and nearly four years after Viv Anderson's breakthrough debut, Regis was selected to make his debut for England at Wembley Stadium against Northern Ireland. Prior to the match he received an envelope through the post containing a bullet. This letter was accompanied with a warning that Regis would receive another bullet if he dared to play at Wembley as a black player in an England shirt.

In 1984, the Jamaican-born John Barnes scored one of England's most memorable goals in a 2-0 victory over Brazil in Rio de Janeiro's Estádio do Maracanã. Just before half-time, Barnes scored England's first goal by weaving and skipping past several Brazilian players, before rounding the goalkeeper and calmly slotting the ball in the back of the net.

Despite scoring a goal which secured a famous victory for England in Brazil, a vocal minority of England supporters stubbornly refused to celebrate the goal as it was scored by a black player. As James Corbett details in his book on the history of the England football team, during the flight from Brazil to the England team's next match in Montevideo, Uruguay, 'four England fans travelling on the same plane as the players continued the abuse by singing racist songs and berating the FA secretary, Ted Croker.'[3]

Attending England international football fixtures at Wembley, and domestic fixtures across the country, was often a hazardous experience for black Caribbean supporters. There was the daunting prospect of fending off personal racist abuse from a vocal minority of white football supporters and watching black players being racially abused by sections of the crowd. Additionally, at some matches, extreme far-right nationalist political organisations, including the National Front, openly attempted to recruit white football fans on the terraces or outside stadiums.

Therefore, for some of the British-born Caribbean population, associating with West Indian cricket, whether they were committed cricket fans or not, possessed a far more desirable appeal than the unappealing notion of supporting the England football team. In addition, supporting football clubs did not usually involve the intimately shared experience of regularly attending matches at stadiums.

Instead, there was a reliance on supporting football clubs from a relatively safe distance. The relationship with football was largely conducted through listening to match commentaries on the radio, watching recorded highlights of matches on television, reading newspaper match summaries and Shoot! magazine, and absorbing reports delivered by white English school, or work, friends and acquaintances who regularly attended matches.

The increasing levels of football-related violence during the 1970s also made some supporters, both black and white, think twice about regularly attending matches at stadiums. Some of the hooligan gangs involved in this violent subculture attached themselves to various football clubs, and a minority of these notorious hooligan gangs, or firms, included high profile black members. West Ham United's Inter City Firm (ICF) hooligan gang was led by Carol 'Cass' Pennant, British-born of Jamaican descent and adopted by a white English family in Kent.

Cass Pennant was to later write a book, also adapted as a feature film, which detailed his upbringing and violent recreational thuggery exploits. As Pennant explains:

> The ICF were no different to other soccer gangs all over the country in our thirst for violence. During the week most of us were law-abiding citizens. Soccer violence was a buzz to us. A buzz so great it took you through every emotion: terror, fear, dread, excitement, elation, a sense of belonging, pride and above all a feeling of sheer power. It was a buzz that gripped you like a drug.[4]

During the 1970s and into the 1980s, some Caribbean youth in Britain were expressing anger and disillusionment towards a lack of opportunities, a sense of social alienation, conflict with extreme right wing political organisations and perceived harassment from inner-city police forces. For some, West Indian cricket offered a powerful representation of black pride, achievement and a direct connection to their Caribbean heritage.

In 1975, the Caribbean diaspora in Britain witnessed the West Indian cricket team triumph in the inaugural World Cup tournament in England. However, the diaspora's relationship with West Indian cricket would experience a more significant set of pivotal issues, events and personalities to respond to during the 1976 West Indies tour.

In 1976, the tenth West Indian team to tour England had recently suffered a comprehensive 5-1 defeat during their 1975/1976 test series tour in Australia. This was largely attributed to the unrelenting and abrasive fast bowling employed by Australia and led by Dennis Lillie and Jeff Thomson, which constantly overwhelmed West Indian batting resistance.

After a series of bruising encounters in Australia, the West Indian captain, Clive Lloyd, was influenced to adopt a similar strategy to the Australians. With Wayne Daniel, Michael Holding and Andy Roberts named in the 1976 tour party for England, the West Indies team possessed a genuine pace attack. These players provided Lloyd with the necessary tools to do the job he demanded. Twenty-six years after the spin bowling guile and artistry of Sonny Ramadhin and Alf Valentine had helped to defeat England at Lord's, it was the relentless speed and hostility of high-quality fast bowling which was entrusted to destroy English batting defences.

A couple of months before the West Indies team arrived in England, this shift in approach was also influenced by Clive Lloyd's disappointment with the attitude and performances of his spin bowlers during the 1976 Indian tour of the Caribbean. In the third test match in Trinidad, India successfully chased down a target of 403 runs to win the match with a second innings total of 406 for the loss of four wickets. The West Indies bowling attack featured three spin bowlers, Imtiaz Ali, Raphick Jumadeen and Albert Padmore.

In response, Lloyd initiated a new focus with an emphasis on fast bowlers on rotation to lead the attack, and encouraged his batsman to unleash a brand of aggressive and powerful batting. This was to be enforced by new levels of professionalism, togetherness and a visible demonstration of regional pride. In Lloyd's opinion, this was necessary to alter the psyche of West Indian cricket which was often viewed as lacking solidity and resolve:

> We didn't want to put on black leather gloves and give clenched-fist salutes, but we did want people to know that we weren't 'Calypso Cricketers' who won or lost with the same carefree smile. What we wanted to show was that from Caribbean territories of just five million people, we could be the best, by ourselves, because of what we had achieved. That was all. Now, if people mistook this for black power, that was their problem.[5]

Clive Lloyd's new vision of West Indian cricket was, therefore, driven by a more disciplined and professional ideal and an emerging sense of black pan-Caribbean pride and assertiveness; with very little room for carefree abandonment. This enhanced sense of professionalism and togetherness was further enhanced by the West Indian team's involvement in the breakaway World Series Cricket tournaments in Australia.

World Series Cricket tournaments were created by the Australian media tycoon, Kerry Packer. From 1977 to 1979, the West Indian players earned substantially more money playing World Series Cricket than they usually received playing cricket for the West Indies/WICB. Garry Sobers acknowledged this as a significant moment when West Indian players were transformed by an improved sense of worth, and a further enhanced sense of professionalism:

> Packer did more for West Indian cricket than he did for any other country because he succeeded in bringing the players together. He made them realise what they could achieve if they played as a team. They understood that if they wanted to win the big bucks, they had to play as a team, regardless of politics or island favours, in order to win the series. This was a chance to earn good money and better themselves. Clive Lloyd took it from there. When they came back into West Indies cricket, they brought that attitude with them. When they asked for improved wages, they knew they had to perform to earn the increase, and were thus more likely to get it.[6]

The diaspora in Britain could now associate with, and be inspired by, a changing culture and attitude in West Indian cricket that coincided with the second decade of independent statehood for many countries in the English-speaking Caribbean region. This era emerged in tandem with a black British Caribbean diaspora, including an emerging British-born second generation, who were attempting to establish their presence in 1970s Britain.

Before the first test match in the 1976 series, the West Indian players received further motivation to test their new approach, beat England and provide a rewarding experience for the British-resident Caribbean diaspora. It came in an interview given by the white South African-born England captain, Tony Greig. The day before the first test match, Greig, with his South African accent firmly intact, was interviewed on the BBC's midweek television sports magazine programme, Sportsnight:

> I'd like to think that people are building these West Indians up, because I'm not sure they're as good as everyone thinks they are. I think people tend to forget it wasn't that long ago they were beaten 5-1 by the Australians and struggled very much to handle them, and only just managed to keep their heads above water against the Indians just a short while ago as well. Sure, they've got a couple of fast bowlers, but really I don't think we're going to run into anything any more sensational than Thomson and Lillie and so really I'm not that worried about them. You must remember that

the West Indies, these guys, if they get on top they are magnificent cricketers. But if they are down, they grovel, and I intend, with the help of Closey and a few others, to make them grovel.[7]

Tony Greig's clearly pre-meditated comments displayed a sense of bravado rarely heard from previous England captains. Greig's plan was to promote the series and get the English press and public onside after recent England defeats. As Greig argues:

The English press seemed to me to have gone out of their way to build up the West Indians and completely write off our chances. I was annoyed by this approach and, in my enthusiasm to drum up some support for England, I simply used an unfortunate word.[8]

Greig refused to hide behind his remarks and attempted to explain himself to the Caribbean community in Britain:

I continued to do my best to try and explain myself. I went to a London radio station that many of the West Indian community used to listen to and did my best to elaborate on what I had been trying to say. I didn't try to hide from anything.[9]

As a South African, Tony Greig may have opted for an aggressive line of verbal attack to demonstrate his nationalistic credentials to be an England cricket captain. However, it was clear that this test series would now be viewed by some in the Caribbean diaspora as a political showdown, and identified as a black-versus-white contest.

The South African government's apartheid system of legal racial segregation and state-enforced discrimination was still in place, despite protests and challenges from South Africa's black and other non-white population. South African international sports teams, including the cricket team, were banned from international competition because of the South African government's discriminatory policies. This was the social and political backdrop to a white South African leading an English cricket team with declared ambitions to defeat a vibrant symbol of black Caribbean unity, West Indian cricket.

As Viv Richards recalls, he watched Tony Greig's statement on a television news programme. As a result, the West Indian players were inspired to respond to the battle lines of race and nationality that Greig's remarks appeared to promote:

Suddenly the news came on about the 'grovel' remark. It simply stunned us. I do not know to this day whether someone was deliberately trying to stir up trouble, strange things like that do happen in test cricket, but somebody told us that the word 'grovel' was often used to put down the blacks in South Africa. Of course, Greig was a South African so that only served to add fuel to our anger. Even if Greig had not been having a dig at us, his remark really worked wonders for us. We were so fired up, it was as if he had unintentionally handed us the ammunition we needed to win the series. And that is what happened.[10]

Tony Greig's comments, with their perceived racist overtones, helped to further galvanise the West Indies team and propelled them to a convincing 3-0 series win. In the final test at The Oval, Greig's reaction to taunting by some West Indian supporters was to briefly 'grovel' on his knees across the outfield. Greig received harsh treatment during the series from some West Indian supporters, although much of it was good natured. His smiling on-pitch 'grovel' performance at The Oval was an entertaining comic display, thoroughly enjoyed and applauded by some of the West Indians in the crowd who had been vocally taunting him. As Greig recalls, 'They (the West Indian spectators) loved it and at the end of the match I had no option, all I could do was crawl off, grovel off myself.'[11]

Viv Richards began and ended his first West Indies test series tour by making two impressive scores. He scored 232 runs in the first innings of the first match at Trent Bridge and 291 in the first innings of the fifth and final match at The Oval in a West Indies first innings total of 687. His score of 291 runs at The Oval was the highest individual score by a West Indian batsman in England. In total, Richards scored 829 runs, despite playing only four out of the five test matches.

Alongside his fellow Antiguan, Andy Roberts, the regular selection of Richards slowly began to broaden the representative spectrum of the West Indies cricket team. The selection of players to represent the West Indies no longer appeared to be restricted to players who were from Barbados, Guyana, Jamaica and Trinidad. By 1985, Viv Richards became the first West Indies captain who was not from one of the 'big 4' Caribbean countries.

Richards' key contribution to West Indian success in England, which included helping to secure the 1975 World Cup victory, enhanced his reputation with some West Indians living in Britain. However, it was not just his uncompromising attitude, visible self-belief and destructive batting style that increasingly cemented this relationship. Some of the West Indian supporters who flocked in substantial numbers to Lord's and The Oval in London, Old Trafford in Manchester, Edgbaston in Birmingham and Trent Bridge in

Nottingham, metropolitan areas in England with a significant Caribbean presence, also responded to Richards' identifiable projection of Caribbean nationalism.

To an extent, Richards' understanding of the black Caribbean diaspora's condition in Britain and its battles against racism was born from experience. During the 1970s, Richards had cause to respond to overt racism while playing for his English county team, Somerset. During a game against Worcestershire, a group of visiting Worcestershire supporters, influenced by a high intake of alcohol, repeatedly sang, 'Viv Richards you are a black bastard.'[12] Richards reacted angrily by leaving his position in the field and waded into the crowd to confront the abusive supporters.

During another match at Headingley in Leeds, Richards, on hearing racist taunts aimed at him by a Yorkshire supporter, demanded that the spectator stand up and show himself. Ian Botham, Viv Richards' close friend, Somerset colleague and sometime England opponent, observed that the Yorkshire supporter in question declined to openly reveal his identity to Richards. In Botham's opinion, the supporter had made a wise decision as, 'Viv would probably have flattened him and finished up on a disrepute charge from the TCCB (the Test and County Cricket Board).'[13]

For some in the Caribbean diaspora in Britain, Richards projected an image of a West Indian who refused to take a backward step in the face of adversity. While living in England during the 1976 test series, Hilary Beckles observed that:

> From the beginning, Richards was businesslike in his demolition of English bowling. His powers of concentration and, above all, his haste made me wonder if he possessed a hidden agenda. It did not matter in the least; his was a level of mastery I had never seen before, and wished to see in all our people's endeavours. I believed that he understood the seriousness of our condition and was prepared to act with all means necessary. We, the wretched of England's inner cities, had never seen the likes of it.[14]

It is conceivable that many of the urban-based British-resident Caribbean diaspora would not have described themselves as being 'the wretched of England's inner cities'. However, Hilary Beckles convincingly describes how Richards' muscular actions on the field of play appeared to complement his approach in representing the Caribbean diaspora in Britain.

The author and journalist, Mike Marqusee, acknowledged Viv Richards' symbolic connection with some of the British-resident Caribbean community. Employed at the time as a youth worker in

London, Marqusee accompanied a group of young men born in the Caribbean, or of Caribbean descent, to the 1983 one day World Cup final at Lord's. It was a match in which the West Indies surprisingly lost to India, despite being installed as firm favourites to emerge as world champions for the third time. Along with the West Indies team's close association with black pride, it was the group's interaction with Viv Richards' image and projected demeanour that provided them with associated self-esteem:

> As we drove to Lord's, our party was in good humour. You could see the sure anticipation of a West Indian victory on the young men's faces and hear it in their jokes and laughter. This was a day to celebrate the black kings of cricket and they intended to savour every moment. After we parked, we walked through the leafy streets past posh houses to the ground, mingling with little bands of West Indian and Indian supporters. Passing a group of turbaned Sikhs in suits and ties, my overgrown charges (they were all bigger than me) swaggered as if each one was Viv Richards strolling to the crease, as if each one partook of the power and majesty of the West Indian side.[15]

Richards asserted an overtly masculine and fearless post-colonial approach to black Caribbean self-identification. His politicised consciousness and nationalist sentiments reflected ideas and themes cemented in black power politics and similar to those expressed by the singer, Bob Marley and by Walter Rodney, the Guyanese political activist, writer and academic. With reference to his refusal to join a representative West Indies cricket team tour of South Africa, while the apartheid system was still firmly in place, Viv Richards stated:

> The whole issue is quite central for me, coming as I do from the West Indies at the very end of colonialism. I do believe strongly in the black man asserting himself in this world and over the years I have leaned towards many movements that follow this basic cause. It was perfectly natural for me to identify, for example, with the Black Power movement in America and, to a certain extent, with the Rastafarians.[16]

This sense of a Caribbean nationalism, evident in the approach taken by Richards, blended with the West Indian team's approach as a representative cohesive unit, further developed the relationship between the team and some members of the diaspora community. The Trinidadian writer and broadcaster Darcus Howe, who arrived in Britain in the early 1960s, observed this connection when it emerged during the 1970s and developed further in Britain during the 1980s:

> There was a very strong nationalist spirit and, because we were
> exiles, those of us in England, particularly in Brixton where I lived,
> felt it most strongly. To see Viv Richards walking out to bat at The
> Oval, which was just down the road, without a helmet, no matter
> how fast the bowler was, and wearing his Rasta armbands of gold,
> green and red was inspirational. This was a time when black
> militancy was building, you had the Brixton riots in 1981 and that
> fed off the swagger and the success of the West Indies side.[17]

The pan-Caribbean nationalist spirit embodied by the West Indian
team fed into a growing sense of collective black Caribbean assertiveness
in Britain. The growing presence of Jamaican reggae, dub and sound
system culture, the influence of Bob Marley's and Big Youth's
politically charged rhythms and vocals, the appropriation of Rastafarian
symbolism and ideology, combined with a spirit of defiance against
hostility, all fed into black Caribbean British youth culture.

In 1979, Jamaican reggae and sound system culture made an
intimate connection with West Indian cricket to produce Cricket
Lovely Cricket, performed by the Jamaican DJ and producer Jah
Thomas. Partly inspired by Lord Beginner's 1950 Victory Test Match
chorus line, this reggae song paid homage to the Sabina Park cricket
ground in Kingston, Jamaica and the cricketing prowess of Michael
Holding and Lawrence 'Yagga' Rowe.

To an extent, the muscular and defiant approach that the West
Indies adopted to confront their opponents on the cricket field,
which continued throughout the 1980s, was being mirrored in
Britain's towns and cities. During this period, demands for social,
economic and political progress from sections of the Caribbean
diaspora in Britain gave rise to social unrest and violent street
disturbances. Weeks after the end of the 1976 test series, London's
Notting Hill carnival became the site of violent confrontation
between groups of, mostly, black Caribbean youths and Metropolitan
police officers.

Then, in 1980, disturbances broke out in Bristol as a result of
worsening relations between the police and members of the black
community. These events were followed in 1981 by disturbances in
Brixton, South London, other areas in London, Toxteth in Liverpool,
Moss Side in Manchester, and other cities and towns in Britain.

The disturbances and violence was seen by some in the West
Indian community as a reaction to perceived over-zealous police
operations, lack of police accountability, social and economic neglect
and racial hostility.

Following the serious disturbances in Brixton, the British government commissioned a report which was led by Lord Scarman. The report concluded in its summary of findings and recommendations that:

> The disorders were communal disturbances arising from a complex political, social and economic situation, which is not special to Brixton. There was a strong racial element in the disorders: but they were not a race riot. The riots were essentially an outburst of anger and resentment by young black people against the police.[18]

In 1982, over 20,000[19] people, the vast majority black, marched from South London to Central London. The march also passed under the eyes of the national media when it went through the centre of London's newspaper industry, Fleet Street. This declared Black Peoples' Day of Action, led by Darcus Howe, was organised to voice discontent against perceived indifference by the Police to investigating the 1981 fire at a party in New Cross, South London, in which thirteen young black people died.

Some West Indian players may have had only a passing interest in notions of black power-style politics. Being infused by a broader sense of professionalism, enhanced from being involved in Kerry Packer's World Series Cricket, was a prime motivator to work hard and win cricket matches. However, the team appeared to take collective inspiration from representing the intense aspirations and frustrations of the Caribbean diaspora in Britain. For some West Indian players, particularly those who did not earn a living on the English county cricket circuit, the intensity of the relationship with some of the Caribbean diaspora in Britain was a revealing experience.

For the Jamaican fast bowler Michael Holding, the 1976 series was his first tour of England as a West Indies player. During a tour match against Surrey at The Oval, Clive Lloyd instructed his players not to chase a final-day target of 239 to win the match. Lloyd preferred that his players got extra batting practice before the start of the test series at Trent Bridge, Nottingham.

This apparent lack of will by the West Indies to pursue victory in a match in England clearly upset some West Indian supporters at The Oval. As play continued on the final day, some West Indian supporters began to heckle the West Indian players. Holding admitted to feeling a sense of confusion and self-confessed naivety. He decided to ask the Barbadian born batsman, Gordon Greenidge, who had lived in England from the age of fourteen, to provide an explanation:

I asked Gordon Greenidge why the fans were being so hostile. He explained how they were desperate for us to win because being a West Indian in a different country could be hard, particularly in England at the time. Most felt like second-class citizens and they wanted to walk around with their heads held high because their countrymen had shown on the field of play what they were capable of. A winning West Indian team meant they didn't have to worry about getting the mickey taken out of them when they went to work.[20]

Gordon Greenidge could certainly talk from informed personal experience about living in England as a migrant from the Caribbean. His personal background differed from his West Indian squad colleagues. Greenidge arrived in England as a fourteen year old schoolboy from Barbados to join his mother who had already settled in Reading, Berkshire. He was the first post-Windrush Caribbean migrant to Britain who eventually emerged as an influential West Indian international cricketer.

Gordon Greenidge learned his trade as a cricketer in English conditions playing on English wickets. By the age of nineteen, he had made his county cricket debut for Hampshire as a promising opening batsman. He continued his development at Hampshire to eventually become part of a potent opening batting partnership with the talented South African player, Barry Richards.

Controversy, bitterness and exile inevitably surrounded West Indian players who established cricketing links with South Africa during its years of apartheid dominated-rule. However, it was not unusual for West Indians playing for English county cricket teams to establish professional relationships with white South African cricketers who they regularly played with. During his career at Hampshire, Greenidge also welcomed his West Indian colleague and fellow Barbadian, Malcolm Marshall and the white South African brothers, Chris and Robin Smith, who both eventually qualified to play international cricket for England.

By the time Gordon Greenidge made his first appearance for the West Indies in India in 1974 at the age of twenty-three, scoring a century on debut, he had also qualified to play cricket for England. Before making his test debut for the West Indies, Greenidge returned to the Barbados for the first time since leaving as a schoolboy to live in England. After continuing to attract the attention of the Barbados team selectors, he was invited to return to Barbados to play for his country of birth in the Caribbean inter-island Shell Shield cricket tournament.

Greenidge's first trip to play cricket in the Caribbean was, overall, not an enjoyable experience. He had to come to terms with his assumption of Barbadian nationality and West Indian identity being forcibly challenged by his fellow Barbadian countrymen. Greenidge was, understandably, unpleasantly surprised by the negative reaction towards him and his identity perceived as an 'Englishman' by some of the Barbadian public. His future as a potential West Indies test cricketer was also under intense public scrutiny:

> I was amazed at the hostile reaction towards me – a sort of racial prejudice in reverse. A typical reaction was: 'Hello, Englishman. What makes you so great?' Those sorts of things hurt me deeply. I could not understand why my own people were turning against me. The abuse continued and worsened whenever I played for Barbados. To help their cause I was not very successful. In six matches I scored only 368 runs at an average of 30 and a hail of abuse greeted me every time I was out. 'Go home, Englishman. Who the hell are you?' It was only later that I realised why they resented me so much. They felt I was taking the place of home-grown players; that I was in a privileged position purely because of a couple of moderate seasons in English cricket.[21]

As well as combating a degree of antipathy from his fellow Barbadians, Gordon Greenidge also revealed a desire to use his cricketing talent to overcome another sense of anxiety and frustration. He outlined how his aggressive, hard-hitting batting technique evolved as a way of releasing his anger as a West Indian living in Britain:

> At times, you felt well, I think I would like to be back in the Caribbean now rather than be here. My anger came out in the way I played. I felt that to forcefully go at what I was doing, to attack, perhaps was a way of letting out that anger. I wouldn't be right to do it to another human being, although you felt like it at times. But I'm going to sure take it out on five and a half ounces. So you just take it out on the ball.[22]

Understanding the, often, intense relationship between the West Indies team and some of the Caribbean community in Britain provided a further source of motivation for Michael Holding, Gordon Greenidge and their colleagues. The sense of togetherness that existed between the players also extended to the diaspora beyond the boundary. The Guyanese batsman, Alvin Kallicharan, recognised the bond between cricket, identity and the Caribbean community in Britain:

In that time in the '70s the support for the West Indies in England was immense. That played a big part in our success. Cricket was their identity and they were desperate to have a successful team in England. Cricket was all they had and that helped us.[23]

When the West Indian team played matches in the Caribbean, the nationality of the majority of spectators was determined by where the team played. This largely separated the units of support at West Indies matches in the Caribbean into Barbadians in Bridgetown, Guyanese in Georgetown, Jamaicans in Kingston, and Trinidadians in Port of Spain.

There was a difference in the West Indian team - Caribbean spectator relationship when the West Indies toured or played in tournaments in England. In England, the West Indies team played to combined sets of West Indian supporters who had migrated from, or were descended from, a variety of British-ruled Caribbean territories. By the early 1970s, many of these territories had also emerged as independent nation states.

Therefore, in Britain, the West Indies cricket team were a Caribbean regional unit which represented a pan-Caribbean diaspora support base. The regional, political and social rivalries between Barbadians, Guyanese, Trinidadians, Jamaicans, Afro-Caribbean and Indo-Caribbean, and other West Indians living in Britain, were temporarily put on hold as the West Indian cricket team, the only symbol of Caribbean regional unification, competed on the field of play.

Jamaican-born Bill Morris became the first black leader of a British trade union when he became General Secretary of the Transport and General Workers union (TGWU) in 1992. After being knighted in 1993, he became known as Sir Bill Morris, later to become Lord Morris of Handsworth when he took up his seat in the House of Lords. Morris, who named his sons Clyde and Garry after Clyde Walcott and Garry Sobers, was appointed as an independent non-executive director of the England and Wales Cricket Board (ECB). As Bill Morris outlines, from a Jamaican perspective, the regional differences between Caribbean people in Britain largely disappeared when West Indians congregated to watch the West Indies play in England:

> From a Jamaican point of view, all barriers were down when we watched the West Indies play cricket. There was a truce and all issues were definitely passed aside. The only marginal debate was within the context of the side. If there were, say, three Bajans (Barbadians) in the team, some of us would think, why couldn't we find a good Trinidadian who was better? Or, why can't we find an equally good or probably better player from Jamaica? There was

always a healthy island or national rivalry, but once the West Indies team stepped on to the green grass, the Jamaican diaspora here (in Britain) was behind the team for all it is worth.[24]

From the 1960s onwards, England versus West Indies cricket matches at The Oval, South London were played in front of large numbers of exuberant West Indian spectators. Many of them were from the nearby district of Brixton which had seen early settlement by Caribbean migrants. By 1955, Brixton had over 1,000 West Indian residents with Geneva and Somerleyton Roads at the heart of this settlement.[25] During the 1960s a visible Caribbean presence had been firmly established.

Before The Oval test match in 1976, an article in The Times newspaper reported that 'The first four test matches have all been accompanied by sounds that would have seemed less strange in West Indies than in England.'[26] Trevor Nelson, a BBC DJ and broadcaster who is British born of Saint Lucian parentage, was with his father at the 1976 Oval test match. In David Tossell's book, Grovel, which explores the events and social issues surrounding the 1976 West Indies tour, Trevor Nelson relived the experience of watching the West Indies at The Oval:

> I never saw black people as happy as at The Oval. People had been lining up to get in but were just clambering over the wall because security was so lax. Some were cooking and selling fried fish and fried chicken in the stands. It was like being in the West Indies. It was like they were dancing on the grave of English cricket.[27]

The first international cricket match I attended in England was in 1980. I was a spectator during the fourth and fifth day of the fourth test match between the West Indies and England at The Oval. I observed how West Indians used cricket grounds in England as a site to re-create a Caribbean match-day setting. In areas of the ground where West Indians congregated whistles were blown, a bell was being rung, and empty beer and soft drink cans and rum bottles were bashed together to create a rhythmic sound. As Jack Williams outlines:

> The black West Indian style of watching cricket was far different from the English tradition with its emphasis on reserve, politeness, passivity and the avoidance of displays of undue passion, though it is not difficult to provide instances when white English cricket crowds have behaved very differently. For African Caribbean spectators, watching cricket has been a means of participating in the match.[28]

At irregular intervals, a battered cassette tape recorder in the stands played a distorted version of a popular reggae/calypso pop song, Who's Grovelling Now? The song was written and recorded by Ezekel Gray, a British-based Jamaican DJ, entertainer and musician. Ezekel Gray, also known as Ezeke or The Man Ezeke arrived in Britain from Jamaica in the 1950s and returned to Jamaica in the 1960s. He came back to live in England in 1975, a year before the record was originally produced and released in response to Tony Greig's grovel remarks. As Ezeke recalls, after being angered by Greig's comments which provided the inspiration to write and perform the song, he developed an unlikely friendship with the man he so gleefully taunted on record:

> I used to go on Nationwide on the BBC (a Current Affairs television programme) and I was the cricket guy. I was the guy who would come on just after the news with a guitar and sing cricket songs whenever the West Indies came over to play. I made the record because I read an article that Tony Grieg said he would make the West Indies grovel. It was as if he was biting into the soul of those of us who were descended from slavery. So people were expecting something and wanted to find out what Ezeke had to say.

> After that I made a record with Tony Greig! And after I made that record, The Daily Express newspaper put us together and came down to Lord's to write an article about us and take pictures. We became buddies in the 70s until he went to Australia. The West Indian community were very excited about Who's Grovelling Now? and I remember during the match at Lord's a guy ran on to the pitch and gave Tony Greig a copy of the record! [29]

During the 1980 tour, despite the fact that Tony Greig's international cricket career had by then ended, the record had experienced a re-birth in popularity as the unofficial West Indian cricket supporters' anthem in Britain. The chorus of Who's Grovelling Now? joyfully teased Greig to a tune, rhythm and style influenced by the song, Who's Sorry Now? made popular in the 1950s by the American singer, Connie Francis:

> Who's grovelling now?
> Who's grovelling now?
> Grieg you're a loser somehow
> If you had your way you would never let us play
> So tell me, who is grovelling now?

Verse four of the song sets out to celebrate West Indian mastery and dominance over those who invented and imported the game to the Caribbean:

Remember you were the teachers in the beginning
You showed us how to play the game
So you are the ones to blame
If you can't find the players to play the game
Go back to school again

Back in 1976, the South-London based producers of the record set up stalls outside Lord's, The Oval and Edgbaston in order to supply demand from West Indian supporters. My friend's father, a mechanical engineer who migrated to Britain from Guyana in the 1960s, attended the 1976 Oval test match with a group of his West Indian work colleagues. On day one, he bought a copy of Who's Grovelling Now? outside the ground.

He triumphantly sang the song with a group of friends on the short underground train journey from The Oval to his home in Balham, South London. Immediately on arrival, he insisted on playing the record on the living room record player for the family to listen to for weeks afterwards.

Some West Indian supporters often adopted an entrepreneurial approach to attending matches by selling seven-inch vinyl records, music cassettes, segments of sugar cane and small plastic-cup portions of rum. Chicken, rice and salad, rum and beer were being shared, consumed, and occasionally sold to each other. According to Steve Stephenson, a Caribbean community leader and lecturer, this ritual of exchanging food and drink at West Indian cricket matches in England helped to confirm positive relationships between various elements of the Caribbean diaspora:

> When I went to cricket here (in England) there was always this
> thing about sharing drink. Somebody would have a bottle of rum
> from Trinidad, somebody would have a bottle of Demerara rum
> from Guyana, somebody would have a Jamaican rum, and
> somebody would have a Cockspur rum from Barbados. We shared
> food and we shared drink. Cricket was important for us because it
> was a social vehicle which kept us together from different islands,
> and we maintained these friendships through cricket.[30]

The more opinionated West Indian groups in the crowd exchanged loud commentary on the progress of the match with nearby England supporters. These animated exchanges were usually good natured but mild abuse was occasionally exchanged as tensions surfaced between some West Indian and English supporters.

Some England players fielding near the boundary ropes, and in front of the majority West Indian areas of the ground, were humorously taunted. Ian Botham, as combative as ever, appeared to enjoy responding to comments from the West Indian contingent. Some of the heckling he received from a section of the crowd included claims that, in their eyes, Ian Botham was not a true friend of Viv Richards.

Players from both teams were often given vociferous advice from some of the West Indians in the crowd, and West Indian players were not immune from crowd barracking as an integral part of the match-day experience. I witnessed a rather heated exchange between some West Indians and the Guyanese batsman, Faoud Bacchus, who was in a fielding position in front of some West Indian supporters seated by the boundary ropes. Towards the end of this battle of words, Bacchus turned to the crowd and suggested that they calmed down.

The noise levels in the West Indian sections of The Oval crowd, and in particular in the stands positioned behind the Harleyford Road, increased with any sign of West Indian success on the field. Towards the end of play on the fourth day, the West Indians in the Harleyford Road section were clearly at their nosiest after celebrating the fall of four English wickets during the early stages of England's second innings.

England ended the final session of day four having scored a total of only twenty runs for the loss of four wickets. The match report in the Daily Telegraph newspaper appreciated the efforts of the English batsmen, Brian Rose and Michael Gatting, for preventing further damaged caused by the bowling of Michael Holding and Colin Croft. The Telegraph report, with a hint of sarcasm in reference to the celebrating West Indian spectators at The Oval, praised the defiant batting of Rose and Gatting as displaying a 'calmness not prevailing among a large but noisy crowd.'[31]

Some young English schoolboy spectators also banged empty drink cans to create improvised percussion noises, and waited for an opportunity to run on to the outfield with their West Indian supporting friends. For them, the West Indian brand of spectator engagement was clearly infectious.

During the 1960 and 1970s, crowd invasions became an established feature of West Indies matches in England. For some spectators, attempting to charge on to the pitch to celebrate a West Indian batsman's century, or the fall of a key English wicket, became a major feature of the day's entertainment. Despite the potential for play to be disrupted and with umpires and players from both teams usually encouraging supporters to return to the stands.

By the end of the 1980s, largely due to improved security measures during matches and slightly more restrained crowd behaviour, invasions were restricted to the end of a match as spectators attempted to congratulate players sprinting off the field, grab stumps and bails as souvenirs, and find a vantage point near the pavilion to cheer or berate players during the post-match awards ceremonies.

At The Oval during the 1973 tour, after Clive Lloyd had reached ninety-nine runs during the first innings of the first test match, a section of the crowd responded by partially invading the playing area. They were convinced that Lloyd had already reached his hundred. The exasperated BBC radio commentator observing these events was keen to describe the disruptive invaders as being both West Indian and English in appearance:

> They're all running on to the field to congratulate him but he's only ninety-nine. He hasn't got his hundred yet! The scoreboard is perfectly clear. It says ninety-nine and Bill Frindall (the BBC cricket match scorer and statistician) is perfectly clear. He says ninety-nine and about a couple of hundred kids have rushed on to the field and congratulated him. What are they going to do when he gets the ton? They're trampling on the wicket a good deal and I might observe, just as a matter of strict fact, that it is a multi-coloured crowd. They are both very black and very white children amongst the culprits but they're mostly children. One or two older boys ought to know a bit better. [32]

When Clive Lloyd eventually reached his hundred, and despite a plea from the PA announcer that spectators should remain in the stands, there was a repeat invasion by a group of overjoyed supporters. One West Indian spectator, clearly satisfied with Lloyd's performance at The Oval, ran up to Lloyd and handed him a celebratory drink of rum and orange juice. [33]

During the third test match of the 1973 series at Lord's, crowd encroachment on the playing area which had celebratory intentions produced some unpleasant scenes. On what turned out to be the last ball of the third day during England's second innings, Geoffrey Boycott was caught, after uncharacteristically playing a hook shot, by Alvin Kallicharan off the bowling of Keith Boyce. The players from both teams attempted to sprint to the safety of the dressing room in order to avoid the onrushing crowd. Some West Indians in their over-zealousness to celebrate Geoffrey Boycott's dismissal surrounded, jeered and jostled Boycott on his way back to the dressing room. At one stage in this unfortunate post-match drama, Boycott prepared to use his bat to ward off further physical contact.

In 1976, a celebratory pitch invasion followed after Michael Holding had cleaned bowled Tony Greig in England's second innings at The Oval. Greig had only scored one run before he was dismissed by Holding. Some West Indian players, including Clive Lloyd, encouraged the West Indian fans to leave the playing area and return to the stands. One of the umpires, Bill Alley, prepared to arm himself with a cricket stump as protection.

According to the other umpire, Dickie Bird, one ecstatic West Indian spectator streamed on to the pitch and handed fifty pounds worth of five pound and ten pound notes to Bird. The spectator insisted that Dickie Bird passed the money on to Michael Holding for taking Tony Greig's wicket. Holding didn't receive the money. As Bird later confessed, 'I said, "Thank you very much, man" and stuffed the notes into my back pocket.' Dickie Bird safely invested the sum of fifty pounds into his Halifax Building Society account.[34]

Cricket grounds provided a public space in which West Indians could congregate and express collective jubilation at events on the field. To an extent, vociferous support for the West Indies to defeat a symbol of English authority, the England cricket team, provided some West Indians with an outlet to 'let off steam' or release feelings of frustration or unfulfilled ambition in Britain. As Bill Morris argues:

> The exuberance among the spectators was almost a sort of release, because if you haven't got a platform and you weren't able to express your view in the council chamber, or in your local council. Because you were not part of real connection with the political process, and your representation in the House of Commons was almost nil. Who speaks for you? Nobody. Then, throwing your hands up and doing a dance on the pitch is probably your way to say we're here, we're alive and we've got a point of view and if you give us a chance we can win something. [35]

Despite the everyday reality of tensions between some members of the Caribbean community and the police, the strain in the relationship was usually put on hold between West Indians and the police at cricket matches. Colin Hutton was a crowd control police sergeant who, during the 1970s, was often in charge of police personnel at West Indies matches at The Oval:

> The fans were good natured, most of the time, and we had a bit of a repartee with them. There was some bad behaviour from time to time but most of the time it was for something like drunkenness. During the day, after drinking rum and Red Stripe beer, the West

Indians became more vociferous. I had no problems with drums being played and whistles being blown as long as it was done in a festive way.

I was once at the Surrey Gates end of the ground doing a ground patrol during a West Indies v Australia World Cup match at The Oval. It was a sunny day and the West Indian supporters were getting boisterous, and one of them lent over and grabbed my hat off my head. After much laughter from the crowd and a few light-hearted comments from me, the helmet was returned. A picture of the incident appeared in The News of the World newspaper, a copy of which I have somewhere in the house![36]

The Oval was not the only ground in England where a vocal West Indian support made its presence felt. As Bill Morris recalls, the West Midlands-based Caribbean community had their own point of assembly during matches at Birmingham's Edgbaston cricket ground:

In those days you could walk down to the ground on the day before a match and buy your tickets. You could also buy your tickets at the ground at the last minute if you wanted to. One West Indian would buy fifty tickets and knew that, within their community, they could sell the tickets or even organise a group. The West Indians used to populate the Hollis Stand and we would be there in large numbers cheering the team along. The atmosphere was wonderful and, at times, the cricket was an interruption to a good day's fun.

This was the occasion when the diaspora could speak to the nation through its cricket. Our voices would be heard and our presence would be seen and recognised sitting in the stands waving the flags and banging our beer cans together and making a statement of arrival. This was more than a cricket match, it had deep psychological messages. We were here, we had arrived and we were competing.

It was a social occasion and a political occasion as well because, during the interval, we would all debate politics as well as any other subject under the sun, and it wasn't just all about what was happening back in the Caribbean. Caribbean people are very knowledgeable about world affairs and we think we have all the solutions to the world's problems! So, in between overs we would also share our intricate knowledge of nuclear missiles, wars, poverty and social degradation.[37]

The bond between cricket and the Caribbean diaspora in Britain was not just limited to the relationship between West Indian players and spectators on match day. The relationship between cricket and the Caribbean community in Britain continued to filter through a national network of West Indian cricket clubs.

Steve Stephenson arrived in Britain from Jamaica in 1971. By 1992, as well as being established as a Caribbean community leader and college lecturer, he helped to create The Victoria Mutual Caribbean Cup. Steve Stephenson was the Chairman and Courtney Walsh, the former West Indian captain and fast-bowler, was the competition's Honorary President. For the last ten years, Stephenson has also been the chief organiser of the annual Winston Davis benefit cricket match in England. Davis, a fast bowler from St.Vincent who played fifteen test matches for the West Indies, is now a wheelchair-user and resident in England after an accident in St.Vincent left him paralysed.

The Victoria Mutual Caribbean Cup was a national competition for West Indian cricket and social clubs in Britain with a Caribbean heritage, including teams from Birmingham, Bristol, Leeds, London and Nottingham. For some years, the competition existed alongside the Clive Lloyd league before eventually folding in 2007.

Other players from various backgrounds and nationalities were welcome, including players with English, Australian, Pakistani and Indian heritage. However, competition regulations stated that in each match, a team had to field at least six players of Caribbean heritage. The aim of this regulation was to ensure a distinct Caribbean presence within all teams throughout the competition.

West Indian cricket clubs have also helped to produce players who have had international cricket careers with the West Indies and England. Stuart Williams from St. Kitts and Nevis and Corey Collymore from Barbados both played for the West Indies and for the Leeds Caribbean cricket club. Devon Malcolm, who later went on to play for Derbyshire, Northamptonshire, Leicestershire and England played for the Sheffield Caribbean club. Chris Lewis played for The West Indian Cavaliers, Nottingham and Alex Tudor has also played for the Cavaliers since retiring from professional cricket in 2009. Michael Carberry, the last player of Caribbean descent to play test cricket for England, spent some of his early years as a cricketer playing for Old Castletonians club in London.

As Steve Stephenson asserts, during the 1970s and 1980s and into the 1990s, Caribbean cricket clubs in Britain continued to provide sites for local community togetherness, as well as opportunities for diaspora communities across the country to compete against each other:

In a cricket club, you'll have forty guys, with say, forty women, so you would have eighty to 100 people in a cricket club. Within that cricket club you'll have people with all sorts of skills. I knew a guy who was a mechanic who would fix my car. I had another guy who was an electrician. We'd all help each other, so the club played an important part. We'd lend each other money and things like that, so it wasn't only about cricket.[39]

Through the established sporting and social vehicle of the cricket club, some West Indians could attempt to replicate the achievements of the West Indian team by taking part in direct competition with English opposition. As part of their annual fixtures commitment, the Leicester Caribbean Cricket Club played a series of Sunday invitational friendly matches in other parts of Leicestershire, Lincolnshire, Southend in Essex and Wales.

According to Earle Robinson, a cultural archivist and a Leicester Caribbean Cricket Club trustee, a couple of humorous incidents occurred on weekend club trips to play teams in Lincolnshire and Wales. Both of these enthusiastic host clubs assumed they were actually playing an official West Indies touring side and hung banners across streets which read, 'Welcome to the West Indies cricket team.'[40]

These contests, as well as providing an opportunity for an enjoyable excursion for players, families and friends, offered West Indians from an urban migrant experience an opportunity to represent a sense of Caribbean collectiveness against cricket teams from suburban, or rural, areas where few Caribbean migrant families had settled. For a club such as the Leicestershire Caribbean Cricket Club, with its ground only a ten minute walk from Leicester's city centre, this involved playing invitational matches against teams in surrounding Leicestershire villages and small towns, including Stoughton, Market Harborough and Barkby.

The social divisions between black, white, urban and rural, West Indian and Englishness, with cricket as the metaphor underpinning these relationships, are captured in the 1986 British feature film Playing Away. One critical summary of Playing Away described it as a film where, 'Britain's race relations and its imperial hangover are boiled down to a game of cricket, played on a village green between the local side and a team from Brixton.'[41]

Caryl Phillips, an author and playwright, who was born in St.Kitts and came to Leeds, Yorkshire at the age of four months, produced the screenplay for Playing Away. Despite a preference for football and the Leeds United team of the 1960s/1970s in particular, as boy growing up in Leeds, Caryl Phillips was also made aware of the deep affiliation his family had with West Indian cricket:

> As a five-year-old, I knew all about Garfield Sobers, Basil Butcher, Seymour Nurse, Wes Hall, Rohan Kanhai, Charlie Griffith, Conrad Hunte and the other players, for in my house these were names that were whispered with an almost biblical reverence. When the West Indies came to play at Headingley in Leeds, the door to the house seemed to be open to a permanent crush of relatives and guests. I remember the excitement as my parents prepared to go out to a celebratory dance at which the players would be present. My own sporting world was dominated by Leeds United and an admiration for Jack Charlton and Billy Bremner. However, I understood that my parents were tolerating, not encouraging, my passion for this inelegant sport. [42]

Directed by the British-based Trinidadian filmmaker, Horace Ové, Playing Away is a comedy infused with light touches of drama. It sets up a clash of opposites through a tale about the visit of a West Indian cricket club, the Conquistadors, to play an invitational match in Sneddington, a fictional village in Suffolk. The Conquistadors from Brixton are a team of first and second generation West Indians in England captained by Willy Boy, played by the Guyanese actor, Norman Beaton. Willy Boy's challenge is to organise a team subtly divided by generational rifts and Caribbean regional rivalries.

Some in Sneddington are perturbed by the prospect of a visit by the Conquistadors, and particularly mindful of recent inner-city disturbances involving some members of the black Caribbean community. A Sneddington resident expresses his anxieties in a village pub before the arrival of the Conquistadors:

> There are drugs to contend with. That's part of their culture. They're liable to burn a few buildings down if things don't go their way. Have you read a paper lately, have you? Watched any tele? That's all there is to see whether you like it or not. Facts are facts. There is no point in burying our heads in the sand! [43]

Despite a state of uneasiness and distrust between the teams and their followers, an off-beat but reasonably harmonious and, occasionally, amorous set of relationships slowly emerge during the build up to the grudge match finale. Willy Boy's pre-match comments to his team are partly influenced by a desire to overcome internal conflicts, and fight back against the negative views of him and his players expressed by some members of the village team. His ambition to achieve personal redemption through victory helps to counteract anxieties about his decision to migrate to Britain and, in turn, the disappearing dream of returning to live in the Caribbean:

> I don't have no big speech or team talk to give or nothing. Everybody have their own idea what we doing here and if we should be here and the rest. But now that we're here, we might as well play, and I mean play. I don't have no time to fool around with these people. A cricket ground aint no place to separate the good from the bad. It is us and them. No gentlemen shit out there. We play, we win and we gone. But mostly, we win. You hear?! [44]

Largely due to a spirit of Caribbean togetherness and a collective desire to dominate their opponents, the West Indian cricket club emerged as victors. The path to success can be attributed to Willy Boy's management of the generational and regional Caribbean tensions within the team. Of course, as a tale of redemption and triumph by outsiders in unfamiliar territory, the film would not have made sense if Willy Boy's team had been defeated.

From 1980 to 1995, the West Indies team dominated international test match cricket by playing twenty-nine matches without losing a series. The only major setback was the unexpected defeat by India in the 1983 World Cup final at Lord's. The Caribbean diaspora were able to witness five West Indian test match tours in England from 1980 to 1995: the West Indies won fourteen test matches to England's four, and were victorious in the 1980, 1984 and 1988 test series.

In 1984, the West Indies won all five test matches in what became known as the 'Blackwash' series. Television cameras captured a West Indies supporter at The Oval holding up a white banner with 'Blackwash' (as opposed to the term 'Whitewash') written in thick black ink. It was a sign that projected the triumphant euphoria of some West Indians who used cricket victories over England as a metaphor for vibrant black success.

However, by the early 1990s a change began in the pattern of West Indian tour results in England. When the 1991 and 1995 series of test matches ended in draws, a brake had been applied by English cricket to the continuous cycle of West Indian series dominance on English soil.

From 1980 to 1995, eleven players born in the Caribbean, or of Caribbean heritage, played for England as test cricketers. Roland Butcher was born in Barbados and migrated to England at the age of thirteen. Butcher was a key member of the 1980s Middlesex team who, with fellow Caribbean born players Norman Cowans, Wayne Daniel,

Wilf Slack and Neil Williams, became known on the English county cricket circuit as 'The Jackson Five' after the African-American family pop group.

Roland Butcher made his England test debut in Barbados during the first match of England's 1981 West Indies tour, and was the first black player to play test cricket for England. After his selection was confirmed, Butcher commented that as a West Indian in 1970s Britain, cricket was one of his few realistic career options:

> There is not a lot of hope for the average black youngster in this country these days with the unemployment situation. The prospects of making progress are slim. They have a feeling they are not going to get on, not going to get an opportunity. I suppose I could have been feeling like that but for cricket. But, I've been given my break, and playing for England must give everybody else encouragement.[45]

From 1980 to 1995, eight other players born in the Caribbean represented England at test level. Norman Cowans and Devon Malcolm were born in Jamaica: Wilf Slack and Neil Williams were born in Saint Vincent; Gladstone Small in Barbados; Phillip DeFreitas in Dominica; Chris Lewis in Guyana; and Joey Benjamin was born in Saint Kitts. Of the two players born in England, David Lawrence is of Jamaican descent and was the first English-born player of Caribbean descent to play test cricket for England. Mark Ramprakash is of mixed Indo-Guyanese and English parentage. Ramprakash, who was also a promising footballer, eventually opted for a career in cricket after signing schoolboy forms to play for Watford football club.

Gladstone Small arrived in Britain at the age of thirteen and played seventeen test matches for England between 1986 and 1991. Small, who works as an ambassador for the Professional Cricketers' Association (PCA), acknowledges the transgenerational connection between Caribbean identity, West Indian cricket and growing up in Britain:

> Cricket was all you had at the time. My parents and the parents of the kids then were very much West Indians. Cricket linked them to the culture they knew and remembered and had brought from home. West Indies cricket was probably the biggest product to leave the Caribbean. The only time you heard the term West Indies was in connection to cricket. It brought the islands together and was a big source of identity for the West Indians who lived in the UK.[46]

> The second generation got the connection with the game from their parents who came up from the Caribbean in the 50s and 60s. They had that deep-seated love for the game and were the ones who

supported the West Indies team. This was a team who were beating everyone around and highlighting something good and positive about the West Indies. Even those who were born here put on their hook to that connection. As the generational gap has widened, those who were born here in the 80s and 90s don't have that love for cricket and the West Indies team. It has, somewhat, dissipated.[47]

This period of sustained West Indian cricket superiority also coincided with an emergence of a more confident and visible second generation black Caribbean British identity. They combined a pride in their ethnicity with an understanding of their social and cultural Caribbean heritage, which was underpinned by an appreciation of their British nationality and influences. Music, sport and slowly emerging first and second generation representation in mainstream local and national electoral politics, provided a platform for a confirmation of arrival and presence.

In 1986, Merle Amory, born in St. Kitts, was appointed the leader of Brent council in North London. Amory became the first black woman to head a local authority in Britain. In 1987, Guyanese-born Bernie Grant and Diane Abbot, who is British-born of Jamaican parentage, entered the House of Commons as elected Members of Parliament (MPs).

In 1994, after being appointed as an independent non-executive director of the England and Wales Cricket Board (ECB), Bill Morris recalled that while growing up in Jamaica he considered, 'the only recommendation for attending school was to learn how to calculate my batting average when I played for the West Indies.'[48]

West Indian cricket provided some of the British born Caribbean generation, who by the 1980s had begun to forge a distinct black British identity, with inspiration and the route to a sense of transgeneration solidarity with the Windrush generation. The common cause of West Indian cricket was enlivened by the force of emerging Caribbean nationalism, the experience of Caribbean collectiveness in Britain and the opportunity to celebrate vibrant black achievement.

The West Indies cricket team, with a distinct sense of regional pride, unity and on-field professionalism, continued to identify themselves with the British-resident Caribbean diaspora. Large numbers of West Indian supporters continued to claim areas of cricket grounds in England during West Indian tours, and in particular The Oval, as their own public social space. However, in the following decades, cricket would experience serious challenges to its importance as a marker of identity for the British-resident Caribbean diaspora.

Chapter 3

THE DECLINE OF WEST INDIAN CRICKET DOMINANCE

West Indian cricket's downward slide, challenges to cricket as a social force and the changing nature of Caribbean identity in Britain

After a period of cricket dominance that lasted fifteen years, the West Indies finally lost a test series when they were beaten in the 1994/1995 Australia tour of the Caribbean. The Australians won two matches, the West Indies one match and one match was drawn. In the final match at Sabina Park, Jamaica, the West Indies suffered an innings defeat. Australia had now ended the West Indies' long run of test cricket superiority.

Nearly twenty years before this reverse on home soil, Australia had soundly beaten a West Indies touring team 5-1 during their 1975/1976 Australian tour. This defeat, in the face of Dennis Lillie and Jeff Thompson's pace-bowling assault, was a major influence on Clive Lloyd's determination to change the nature of the West Indian cricketer's character and performance, and to reflect a resolute spirit of Caribbean regional cohesion.

In 1996, an even more devastating blow to the soul of West Indian cricket was delivered during the World Cup hosted by India, Pakistan and Sri Lanka. In India, the West Indies were comfortably beaten by Kenya. In response to Kenya's total of 166 runs, the West Indies were bowled out for a disappointing total of ninety three runs during the thirty fifth over of a fifty overs per team competition.

According to Hilary Beckles, the test series defeat at home by Australia, and the World Cup thrashing administered by Kenya, was not just attributable to outstanding performances by the opposition and poor team performances by the West Indies. At the root of these defeats was confirmation of the changing patterns of approach, character and attitude of West Indies cricket, and the looming prospect of long term decline:

> The Sabina Park defeat, and the Kenya routing, confirmed that the question of players' increasing alienation from traditional sources of motivation and pride was no longer controversial. Defeat at the hands of both the strongest and the weakest challengers signalled furthermore that the ethos of professionalism, and its supportive nationalist mentalities, were no longer guiding forces in West Indian cricket.[1]

Brian Lara's image in the eyes of some of his admirers was altered by his response to defeat by Kenya. He was quoted by an Indian reporter as stating to the celebrating Kenyan players that losing to their team was not as painful as it would have been against South Africa.[2] Lara, a future West Indian captain and record-breaking run scorer, had reportedly assessed that losing to an African team (the Kenyan cricket squad were a collection of players of African and Asian heritage) was less of an issue than losing to a white-majority South African team, associated by some West Indians with the legacy of the apartheid-dominated years in South Africa.

Lara later attempted to put his remarks into context and explained to Wes Hall, the West Indies team manager, that 'What I said was that the defeat of Kenya was not as humiliating as when we lost to South Africa in the last World Cup. At the time, South Africa has just come of apartheid'.[3]

The image of West Indian cricket being in decline and in a generally disorganised state has also not been helped by a catalogue of disputes between West Indian players and the much maligned West Indian Cricket Board (WICB). In 2009, West Indian cricketers, represented by the West Indian Players Association (WIPA) led by the former West Indian player, Dinanath Ramnarine, refused to play in a home series of matches against Bangladesh.

This was an unfortunate outcome to a bitter contract dispute between WIPA and the WICB. As a result, a seriously weakened West Indies team was led into the series by a captain, the Barbadian Floyd Reifer, who had not played test cricket for ten years. Unsuprisingly, the West Indies were comfortably beaten by Bangladesh in both test matches and the one day series.

The motivations of recent generations of West Indian cricketers have, arguably, been influenced by wider significant social, economic and political developments. Evolving since the end of British colonial rule and the establishment of independent Caribbean nation states, these changes are firmly embedded in the present day economic and cultural realities in the region. As Sir Trevor McDonald, the British-based Trinidadian broadcaster and writer, convincingly argues:

> The Caribbean has changed so much in the past 20 years. It's no longer an outpost of the (British) empire; it's much more international. You've got a Chinese company building the new pavilion at the Grenada cricket ground, Hugo Chavez selling Venezuelan oil to Jamaica, and the Cubans allowing West Indians to use their healthcare system. All those things have an effect on people's perspective. Do Brian Lara or Shivnarine Chanderpaul, for example, feel the same sense of political identity as Clive (Lloyd) and Viv (Richards) did when they played? I don't think they do.[4]

The perceived attitude portrayed by some West Indian players that they are much more inspired by professional self-interest than regional nationhood, and express limited commitment to represent the ambitions of their public, in addition to reports of continuous mis-management by the WICB, has had an impact on the British diaspora's relationship towards West Indian cricket.

Professor Clem Seecharan, the Guyanese cricket writer, academic and Head of Caribbean Studies at London Metropolitan University, strongly suggests that it is difficult to separate the connection between developing social, cultural and political attitudes towards cricket in the Caribbean and the diapora's attitudes towards West Indian cricket in Britain:

> A shift in a cultural sense of gravity is taking place in the Caribbean environment as well as the environment here (in Britain). What is happening in the region itself has an impact on the team and attitudes created towards West Indian cricket, and that certainly has an impact here (in Britain) as well. People who have been great followers of West Indian cricket, including those who were born in the Caribbean and migrated here in the 50s, the 60s and the 70s, they watch what is happening in West Indian cricket in the Caribbean.

> They see that when a test match is going on in the Caribbean now you have one man and his dog in the ground. Unless England are touring the West Indies and then you have English tourists attending these games. Up to 90% of the people attending these games could be English tourists, especially in Barbados, St Lucia and Antigua, as this is all tied up with tourist business and the way these games are promoted. The results have been an important factor but there is a major change culturally in the region and that change is an orientation towards African American culture.[5]

Since the 1990s, West Indian cricket fans in Britain who had celebrated success during the 1970s and 1980s, had to reconsider a relationship with the West Indies team that no longer seemed to offer a source of pride and inspiration. Evidence of the slowly deteriorating relationship between the diaspora and West Indian cricket can be observed by the decreasing numbers of West Indians attending West Indies matches in England.

Between 2000 and 2009, the West Indies toured England on four occasions. In 2000, England won the test match series 3-1; in 2004, England beat West Indies 4-0; in 2007, England beat West Indies 3-0; and in 2009, England beat West Indies 2-0. Before the start of the 2012 home series against Australia in the Caribbean, the West Indies were officially ranked seventh out of the nine international test match playing nations, and eight out of the thirteen nations who play one day international match cricket.[6]

From a West Indian perspective, the only major respite from this period of underachievement on English soil was the victory against England in the 2004 ICC Champions Trophy final at The Oval. In the Caribbean against England, the outstanding individual West Indian performance was delivered by Brian Lara, who reclaimed his record of setting the highest score in test cricket; hitting 400 not out in the fourth Test in Antigua during England's 2004 tour. However, England won the test series 3-0. The match in Antigua was the only match in the series that England failed to win as it ended in a draw. It was England's first test series win in the Caribbean since 1968.

In 2009, the declining importance of West Indies tours for the English cricket authorities, players and spectators was confirmed. The West Indies were third choice as opposition for this particular series which, as in 2007, and unusual for a West Indian tour, began in May. The West Indies arrived in England as replacements for Sri Lanka. The Sri Lankans declined to tour England after initially agreeing to replace Zimbabwe.

Before the West Indies arrived in England, there was some cause for optimism from those in the Caribbean diaspora in Britain still concerned with the affairs of West Indian cricket. The 2009 England tour of the Caribbean, which had just ended two months before, had seen the West Indies beat England 1-0 in a five test series.

The West Indies captain, Chris Gayle, arrived in England from South Africa just two days before the first test match at Lord's, after fulfilling his lucrative contractual obligations to represent the Kolkata Knight Riders in the Indian Premier League (IPL). The Barbadian fast-bowler, Fidel Edwards, arrived in England three days before the match after playing for the Deccan Chargers in the IPL.

With the English team, supporters and media looking forward to a competitive Ashes test series against Australia later on that summer, the West Indies gave the appearance of offering themselves as a warm-up act before the English summer's main cricket attraction.

I attended the first day of the first test match at Lord's on a Wednesday morning. Not having a traditional Thursday morning start immediately gave the day a slightly surreal and anti-climatic feel before a ball had been bowled. The West Indies won the toss and invited England to bat first. The Wisden Cricketers' Almanack report of the first day's play referred to the late arrivals of Chris Gayle and Fidel Edwards, and the lack of warm-up games in April and May, as contributing to the team's performance on the field. The Wisden report indicated that 'perhaps of this, the tourists looked unfocussed and unprepared, and they dropped six catches, two of them sitters, during the first day's final session to let England off the hook.'[7]

The Caribbean Steel Band international, a four-man steel band turned out in smart matching red shirts, were drafted in to play some calypso rhythms near the refreshments area during the lunch and tea intervals. However, there were few West Indians in a healthy, but not full capacity, crowd to engage in this attempt to create a Caribbean carnival spirit on a bright but breezy North London afternoon.

As play progressed, I successfully identified a small group of up to thirty West Indian spectators who had converged in front of one of the main scoreboards. They could just about be seen and heard when a West Indian bowler claimed an English wicket. The loudest collective shrill from this group came when Kevin Pietersen was out for 0, caught by the wicket-keeper, Denesh Ramdin, off the bowling of Fidel Edwards. Despite's Edwards' admirable first innings performance in which he claimed six wickets, England beat the West Indies within three days at Lord's. England also comfortably won the second test match at Durham.

The last fixture of the 2009 tour was a one day international match at Edgbaston, Birmingham. England easily beat the West Indies by a margin of fifty-eight runs. After the match, the former England cricket captain and now journalist, Mike Atherton, concluded that:

> There was no glory to be had and there were not that many West Indies supporters in the ground, although there were a few, given the large numbers who live in and around Birmingham. Not many of them voiced their displeasure, though; perhaps they have become

immune to failure or maybe they have just taken their cue from the players, whose indifference from the start to the finish of this tour was palpable.[8]

While the failure of the West Indies to inspire has led to a reduced level of support from the diaspora in Britain, other factors have also influenced their reluctance to attend West Indies matches in England. There has been an unwillingness by some West Indians in Britain to conform to spectator regulations at English cricket grounds. Frank Birbalsingh identified the conflicting ways in which West Indian and English spectators expressed themselves while interacting with events on and off the cricket field:

> There is a world of difference between a quiet, picnic lunch of dainty cucumber sandwiches and tea on the manicured lawn of an English test ground, and the spicy patties and hot-flavoured delicacies loudly advertised, and openly peddled by a host of competing vendors on West Indian cricket grounds. This is not to mention bottles or rum and beer to wash down the food, nor the gay rowdiness of a contradictory and improbable atmosphere heightened by fits of outlandish laughter, scurrilous banter, outbursts of ribaldry, violent arguments and heated debates about everything and nothing.[9]

As Jack Williams notes, by the end of the 1980s, English cricket authorities judged it was time to respond:

> By the 1970s and 1980s many English whites were far more critical of the conduct of West Indian spectators than they had been in 1950. In 1976 an article in The Cricketer asked whether it was 'really beyond the wit of ground authorities to put a stop, by "conditions of entry", confiscation of instruments, or even mobilisation of public opinion, to the jungle drumming and other non-cricket noises that must surely exasperate thousands of paying spectators and hundreds of distant watchers. They might begin by calling for a couple of doctors to certify the man with the whistle.'[10]

The revelry, humour, passion and noise that West Indian supporters brought to cricket grounds in 1970s and 1980s, which inevitably increased in volume with West Indian successes on the field, have been largely thwarted by the English cricket authorities. By the early 1990s, rules and regulations were in place in most of the major test match venues that made drums, horns, whistles, flags, flaxons and banners more difficult to bring to a West Indies cricket match in England. By

2011, the Lord's cricket general ground regulations for spectators attending matches included:

> No betting (unless specifically authorized by the MCC Committee), unnecessary noise, or confusion of any kind is permitted in any part of the Ground. Flags, Banners, Musical Instruments, Klaxons, Rattles, Fireworks and other articles which may constitute an annoyance to spectators are also prohibited inside the Ground. The wearing of Fancy Dress costumes and oversized hats inside the ground is prohibited.[11]

Regulations which govern spectator behaviour at matches in England may vary from one cricket ground to another. For example, on day four of the 2011 England v India test match at the Edgbaston, spectators were encouraged to attend the match in fancy dress. Spectators in the Hollis Stand were entertained by the sight of a man fancy dressed as a banana, being enthusiastically chased across the stands by another group of men dressed in gorilla outfits.

Regulations governing spectators are also generally more relaxed for one day and 20/20 international matches. However, West Indian supporters have been notable by their absence at grounds in London, Manchester, Birmingham, Leeds and Nottingham, where they had previously attended matches in large numbers. This decrease in a substantial West Indian presence was observed by Viv Richards. His assessment concludes that rules and regulations introduced at grounds, 'has a big effect and helped to take away the true support we used to get when we came to England.'[12]

Eaton Gordon is British-born of Jamaican parentage and works as a Deputy Sports Development Officer and Warwickshire Cricket Board Community Officer. He is also the Head Coach of Handsworth Cricket Club in Birmingham. According to Gordon, there is a connection between the ground rules governing spectator behaviour which has affected the atmosphere and, therefore, the number of West Indians prepared to attend matches:

> Every time we went to see the West Indies play cricket it was like an outing and you'd get everyone there. And they would all go to cricket, not just to watch the cricket but for the atmosphere. As a youngster, when you woke up in the morning to go to a cricket match, it wasn't just about watching cricket. It was about meeting other families and other kids you knew, having a good time and having a bit of fun. It was like a family picnic and we'd prepare food, take it in, and dish it out. The men would get involved in

drinking their beer, banging their beer cans and talking cricket. Now, the game is more for the purists who are really into cricket and that's when the others started to filter out.[13]

By contrast, the 1994 England tour of the West Indies saw increasing numbers of English cricket fans keen to be involved in the revelry, crowd participation and rhythm largely absent from cricket grounds in England. During the fourth test match in Barbados there appeared to be more English supporters in the Kensington Oval than Barbadians. Some of the England supporters were clearly in a boisterous mood and intent on enjoying the sight, sounds and atmosphere of cricket in the Caribbean.

Many of the English supporters tied England and Union Jack flags on fences around the ground, and wore replica football shirts of the football teams they supported. Some of these flags were proudly emblazoned with the towns and cities they came from and the football teams they supported, including Burnley, Clevedon and Derby County. When Alec Stewart reached his second century of the match, groups of ecstatic Englishmen jumped over the boundary ropes, sprinted across the outfield and danced with joy, including bare-chested supporters in shorts eagerly clutching bottles of beer.

Apart from Stewart's two centuries, English supporters were also keen to celebrate England's achievement in being the first team to beat the West Indies at the Kensington Oval, Barbados since 1935. The Wisden Cricketers' Almanack reported that the match in Barbados had, 'attracted capacity crowds, swelled by about 6,000 holidaying England supporters, creating a unique and strangely bipartisan atmosphere for a Caribbean test.'[14]

Since the 1990s, travel and tour packages, specifically aimed at English cricket enthusiasts, have significantly increased the numbers of English fans attending matches at Caribbean cricket grounds during England tours. Ben Dirs, a BBC sports journalist, wrote a book outlining the history and exploits of the drinking, chanting and fancy dress wearing Barmy Army faction of travelling English supporters. Ironically, it is now English cricket fans, in the guise of the Barmy Army and those who appreciate their more vociferous spectator involvement, who present a challenge to those at English grounds who prefer a more traditionally English approach to watching cricket.

Dirs suggests that by the time England toured the Caribbean in 1997/1998, the Barmy Army had been in existence for three years and 'thousands descended on Jamaica for the first test at Sabina Park, with many England fans confident of a first series win in the West Indies for thirty years.'[15] Unfortunately, for the expectant Barmy Army and the rest of the English travelling support, the West Indies won the six match series 3-1.

Coinciding with the effects of ground rules and regulations, as Mike Phillips argues, the cricket ground as an essential meeting place for the British-resident Caribbean diaspora has slowly decreased in importance:

> In a sense, we don't need cricket any more and that's the problem. We desperately needed it during the 50s, 60s and 70s because there was nothing else that spoke to us. When we went to the cricket ground, and when the West Indies came on tour, you would meet all your friends and it was like carnival for a bit. At The Oval you would always meet people. You would even meet people you hadn't seen for years on the tube on the way to the match. After that, as time progressed, it stopped mattering. If you wanted to meet your friends you could meet them anywhere.[16]

Alongside its declining role as a site for diasporic togetherness, cricket has failed to filter down to the third and fourth generations of the diaspora. For the current descendants of the Windrush generation, the attachment to cricket has been replaced by a devotion to other sports, including football, basketball and athletics. The glamour and increasingly high profile of English Premier League football has become their main focus of attention.

During the 1990s, the appeal of football for the black Caribbean diaspora in Britain was, partly, driven by the formation of the English Premier League in 1992, which replaced the Football League's first division championship as the top tier of English professional football. When Sky beat ITV for the first Premier League live broadcast deal in 1992, they paid £191 million over the following five years for broadcast rights.[17] By 2009, Sky reportedly paid in excess of £1.6 billion to show Premier League matches from 2010-13. Months later, Manchester United's manager, Alex Ferguson, warned of television having too much control of English football because of the amount of money it provides.[18]

The Premier League's prestige and global commercial appeal, including an increasingly loyal following in the Caribbean, has seen football confirm its place as Britain's dominant sporting force. The widening appeal of the England national football team, and the increasing levels of high-profile black players in the English domestic football scene, has also appealed to Britain's black Caribbean population.

The third and fourth generation, British born of Caribbean descent, have become more assured, and at ease, with embracing a sense of Britishness and, indeed, Englishness as an integral part of their personal identity. Therefore, supporting England at football has become an increasingly popular choice.

I watched the 1990 England versus Germany World Cup semi-final, featuring Paul Gascoigne's tears and England's dramatic penalty kick shoot-out defeat, on television with some England-supporting, second generation Jamaicans in a flat in Brixton, South London. It was the first time I had shared the experience of supporting England at football with a group of people of Caribbean descent in Britain.

Fourteen years later, after the 2004 European Football Championships (Euro 2004) in Portugal, the increasing Caribbean diaspora trend towards supporting England was noted by Rodney Hinds:

> Away from the social reasons, in simple terms, life has moved on. Football has taken over. Dwight Yorke was plucked from obscurity in Tobago and has a fairy-tale career with Manchester United. There was a time when we wouldn't openly support England at football. Now, with Sol Campbell and Ashley Cole involved, we do. The West Indian community wanted England to win Euro 2004, but when it comes to cricket there is not too much relateability.[19]

In 1995, Paul Ince, British born of Barbadian parentage, became the first footballer to captain the full international England team. In 2008, as manager of Blackburn Rovers, Ince became the first British-born black manager of a team in the highest tier of English football. It was a landmark appointment, despite his term at Blackburn ending in being sacked after only six months.

Ian Wright, who is British-born of Jamaican parents, had a football career during the 1980s and 1990s which featured memorable performances for clubs including Crystal Palace, Arsenal and West Ham. His goal-scoring exploits also earned him international recognition for England. After he retired from football, Wright's effervescent personality and urban persona helped him to secure a career as a television and radio presenter. Rodney Hinds describes Ian Wright as being responsible for propelling the image of the black footballer 'into the hearts and minds of the football fraternity, both black and white',[20] and becoming 'an urban hero to whom the youngsters on the street could relate.'[21]

The global profile of black Britain is largely projected through the England team's black and mixed-race players. The England team's twenty-three man squad for the 2010 World Cup in South Africa featured nine players of Caribbean descent. Rio Ferdinand, born in England of a St Lucian father and an English mother, was appointed the first non-white captain of an England World Cup squad. Unfortunately for Ferdinand, injury prevented him from playing in the tournament.

During the 2011/2012 football season there were some incidents which placed the issue of racism in English football under increased media scrutiny. Liverpool's Uruguayan star, Luis Suarez, refused to shake Patrice Evra's hand during the pre-match handshake ritual before a Premier League match between Liverpool and Manchester United. Suarez had just returned from serving an eight game ban after racially abusing the Senegalese-born French international player, Evra, during a match between the two teams earlier in the season.

Oldham Athletic's Tom Adeyemi, of mixed English and Nigerian parentage, tearfully reacted to being allegedly racially abused by a supporter at Liverpool's Anfield stadium. This was followed, some weeks later, by a Manchester United supporter at United's Old Trafford stadium charged with aiming racist abuse at Stoke City's Trinidadian footballer, Kenwyne Jones.

The supporter was eventually found guilty of a racially-aggravated public order offence, fined £200 and ordered to pay a £15 victim surcharge and £85 court costs. He was also punished by being banned from entering a football ground in England and Wales for three years, and ordered to surrender his passport when the England national team plays international matches abroad.[22]

Despite these widely reported incidents, overt anti-black racism in English football stadiums has markedly decreased since the 1970s/1980s. For the majority of black football supporters, many football stadiums in English have become less hostile environments, and black footballers have continued to flourish at the vast majority of English professional football clubs. In turn, becoming a professional footballer in England, and Scotland, has become a highly desirable career path for black players, who are British-born, Caribbean-born, from Africa, South America or other countries in Europe.

Top English international cricketers, some of whom also perform in the Indian Premier League, can now earn more money than in previous years. Andrew 'Freddie' Flintoff, who retired from playing professional cricket in 2010, and Kevin Pietersen, have earned considerable sums and been elevated to high-profile celebrity status. However, rising incomes from media rights, sponsorship and merchandising sales have helped football clubs fund increasingly substantial salaries for the vast majority of footballers in the English Premier League.

In 2009, as a 20 year old, Theo Walcott, whose father is of Jamaican descent, signed a new and improved contract with his club, Arsenal. The deal reportedly earned him a salary of £60,000 a week.[23] At the age of 17, Walcott was also the youngest player to be selected for an England World Cup squad. In 2006, he travelled with the squad to the World Cup in Germany but did not play in any of the matches during the tournament. As Devon Marshall, the Jamaican-born ex-England test cricketer, argues:

> If you look at the Premiership and the England team, there are so many black players, and so there are so many black kids playing football. Kids are influenced by big stars, big money and all that business. When they can see Theo Walcott going to the World Cup aged 17, kids start gravitating that way - they want to play football. It's the big money sport, the celebrity sport.[24]

In the 2011 edition of the annual top 100 'rich list' of current and former British and Irish sportsmen produced by the Sunday Times newspaper, fifty-one sportsmen were connected with football while only two were associated with cricket. The cricketers listed were retired former England international players, Phil Edmonds and Matthew Fleming, who were reported to have amassed their wealth through combinations of 'cricket and mining' and 'cricket and finance' respectively.[25]

For the majority of the current descendants of the Windrush, there is more connectivity with West Indian athletes than cricketers, with the Jamaican sprinter, Usain Bolt, firmly established as the world's most famous Caribbean global sporting personality. In rugby union, a sport not traditionally associated with the Caribbean diaspora in Britain, the Trinidad-born Armitage brothers, Steffon and Delon, have both represented the England national team. The British gymnast, Louis Smith, whose father is Jamaican, won a bronze medal at the 2006 Olympic games in Beijing, China.

Lewis Hamilton, whose father is of Grenadian descent, is now a global personality in another sporting discipline, Formula One car racing, which has previously had very little connectivity with Britain's Caribbean diaspora. As Rodney Hinds asserts, these evolving generational shifts in sporting affiliations, away from cricket, should be appreciated and readily understood:

> People of my generation understand how it was, but how it was is not how it is now. I have accepted that and I'm now in sport on a professional basis and I have seen changes. I have a Lewis Hamilton now who I report on. Now a black man in motor sport twenty years

ago was unthinkable. Never mind a black man who is very good at what he does. So, it is about change and, particularly, it's about embracing that change.[26]

As cricket continues to face intense competition from football, basketball, athletics and other sports, it has failed to connect with the majority of the British-born Caribbean diaspora. Paul Weekes, born in London to a father from Montserrat and an English mother, played professional cricket for Middlesex from 1990 to 2006. Weekes argues that the recent crop of West Indian players have failed to inspire the third and fourth generation Caribbean diaspora in Britain:

> Most youngsters are impressionable and follow things which are fashionable and exciting. The West Indian team in the last 10 to 15 years has been none of the above. There is nothing there which is appealing. My dad is from Montserrat. Viv Richards and Andy Roberts are family friends. So when I was growing up I followed West Indian cricket when the team was dominant and exciting with Viv Richards and Michael Holding. Everybody wanted to bat like Viv Richards and bowl as fast as Michel Holding. The closest you get now to a decent West Indian cricketer is Chris Gayle.

> There is nothing eye catching about the West Indies team if you watch them. As a youngster watching them on TV, there is nothing to entertain and excite you. Why should they jump up and celebrate a West Indian team that keeps on losing? There are no heroes and no icons and when you watch the West Indies play at home in the Caribbean on TV, the stadiums are empty. If I put on my TV and watch Arsenal (football club) play, I'll probably find six or seven black players on each side.[27]

At the beginning of 2012, Shivnarine Chanderpaul still held the record of test match appearances (137) for the West Indies. His record of twenty five test centuries is an achievement which has to be respected, as well as his willingness and determination to bat and occupy the crease to save the West Indies from crisis situations. Chris Gayle, who in 2010 scored 333 in an innings against Sri Lanka during his last West Indian tour, arguably, still has the profile and dominant playing ability to become an influential West Indian cricket personality. This potential development largely rests on the strength of the compromise reached between Chris Gayle and the WICB. Following an ongoing bitter dispute with the WICB, Gayle finally agreed to make himself available for selection for the three one day internationals and the 20/20 match during the 2012 West Indies tour of England.

Apart from Gayle and Chanderpaul, who has had his own series of disagreements with the WICB, it's a struggle to identify players amongst the current generation of West Indian cricketers who could become long-lasting and inspirational iconic figures for the British Caribbean diaspora and beyond. As Bill Morris argues, a combination of indifferent performances and substantial admission fees has also strongly influenced the decrease in commitment from the diaspora to West Indies cricket:

> I don't think you can overlook the performances of the team. People like to back success. Who wants to pay £50, £60, £70 for a ticket and see your team lose? It's not just about the end result. You want to see effort for your money. The last time the West Indies toured England (in 2009) they were heavily criticised and the team is not performing in a way which attracts the uncommitted. Only the diehards, from a Caribbean point of view, will go and see them.[28]

Ironically, some of the more optimistic noises about the future of West Indies cricket have been voiced by an Englishman. In 2010 and 2011, Toby Radford, a cricket coach, re-located to the Caribbean and worked with the WICB to set up a high performance centre in Barbados. As Radford confidently predicts, some of the emerging talent from the centre could make a positive impact:

> There's a big, strong quick bowler from Trinidad called Shannon Gabriel, and he can bowl up around 90mph. He's raw but they might want to blood him on a tour of England. They also had a left-arm swing bowler called Delorn Johnson and I can see him coming (to England) because he would suit the conditions. The other thing they have is high-quality spinners. Veerasammy Permaul from Guyana is an exceptional left-armer. Batting-wise, there's Nkrumah Bonner, Devon Thomas and Kieran Powell. There's four or five of the High-Performance Centre team that we had who are really knocking on the door.[29]

While there has been a general retreat from cricket and a lack of intimate association with a struggling West Indies team, the third and fourth generation Caribbean diaspora have also largely failed to transfer their support to England. This is also illustrated by the decline in the numbers of players of Caribbean descent playing county cricket in England and, thus, available to represent the England team.

From 1980 to 1995, eleven players born in the Caribbean, or of Caribbean heritage, made their debuts for England as test cricketers. During England's 1990 tour of West Indies three Caribbean born players, Devon Malcolm, Gladstone Small and Phillip DeFreitas provided the core of the England's pace bowling attack. In England's 1994 Caribbean tour, Chris Lewis, who was born in Guyana, took the match winning wicket by clean-bowling Curtly Ambrose in the West Indies second innings to claim a historic victory for England in Barbados.

From 1995 to 2010, only four players of Caribbean heritage made their debuts for England as test cricketers. All of them were British born. Mark Butcher and Dean Headley are of mixed English and Jamaican parentage. Headley's father, Ron, and grandfather, George, both represented the West Indies at test cricket level. Alex Tudor is of Barbadian parentage and Michael Carberry is of Guyanese and Barbadian parentage.

In March 2010, Carberry was the first player of Caribbean descent to make his test match debut for England since Alex Tudor in 1998. He opened the batting with Alistair Cook and scored thirty and thirty-four in his two innings against Bangladesh. When Michael Carberry's selection for the 2010 tour of Bangladesh was confirmed, Simon Wilde, The Times newspaper cricket correspondent, suggested that 'Carberry's emergence could play a vital part in arresting a decline in Afro-Caribbean cricket in England that reflects the sport's fragile footing in inner-city areas.'[30] Despite Simon Wilde's optimism, Michael Carberry has not represented England since his debut.

Although now fully recovered, a serious illness towards the end of 2010 contributed to Carberry stepping back from the game. During his return to cricket in the 2011 English season, Carberry impressed in a match for his county, Hampshire, by hitting an unbeaten 300 not out in a Championship Division One match with Yorkshire.

Alex Tudor, who is now a professional cricket coach, is confident that Carberry has the ability to play for England again but might struggle to attract the attention of the England selectors. However, in Tudor's opinion, if Carberry became an established England cricketer it would have a positive impact:

> It will be hard for him but his figures over the last three years have been good and he's scored runs. The problem is that he can't get ahead of the captain and vice-captain, (Andrew) Strauss and (Alastair) Cook, who open the batting. Michael has been typecast as an opening batsman but he can bat further down the order and he saves runs with his fielding. If a black guy sees Michael as a role model at the top, and especially a South London boy like Michael who has done well, it might just help.[31]

In addition to the lack of players of Caribbean descent in contention to represent England, there are also very few West Indian international cricketers regularly playing on the English major county cricket circuit for the diaspora in Britain to draw inspiration from. Few English counties are willing to offer long-term professional contracts to the small number of talented and available players from the Caribbean.

The Leicester Caribbean Cricket Club is one of the Caribbean organisations in Britain with a tradition of being involved in events featuring visiting West Indian touring teams. From formal civic receptions organised at Leicester city centre hotels in the 1950s/1960s to 2009, when the West Indian touring team met with Leicester Caribbean Cricket Club members and friends at a more informal reception held at Leicester's African Caribbean centre. Despite the consistency of a relationship with West Indian touring teams, there are now limited opportunities for the club to engage with West Indians playing professionally for their local county cricket club, Leicestershire. This has clearly disappointed Earle Robinson, a Leicester Caribbean Cricket Club trustee:

> When West Indian players used to play for Leicestershire, like the
> fast bowler Andy Roberts, they used to come up to Ethel Road (the
> Leicester Caribbean Cricket Club ground), do some coaching and
> have a drink with the guys. We had a young lad called Lionel Baker
> (a West Indian cricketer from Montserrat) who had a couple of
> trials with Leicestershire. We have a lot of people here in Leicester
> from Montserrat so he spent some time with the Montserrat people.
> When Phil DeFreitas played for Leicester he was very supportive.
> He used to come down and hand out tips, bowl and help out. We
> just don't have players of that calibre any longer. In that way, the
> connection between the West Indian players and the community
> doesn't exist because we don't have the players in the county league
> anymore.[32]

In 1980, there were eighteen Caribbean born cricketers registered to play for the seventeen major English cricket counties during the 1980 season. Of these players, ten had played international cricket for the West Indies.[33] The number of major English county clubs increased to eighteen in 1991 when Durham were granted first-class status. By the time the 2011 edition of The Cricketer's Who's Who annual statistical guide to the English cricket season was published, only two West Indian international cricketers, Kieron Pollard (Somerset) from Trinidad and Gareth Breese (Durham) from Jamaica, were listed in the guide as playing for a county during the 2011 season.[34]

Colin Croft, the former West Indian fast bowler and now BBC cricket analyst, who also played English county cricket for Lancashire, has expressed a sense of disappointment in this continuing trend by arguing that:

> The fact is there are so few West Indians playing for counties these days that one really has to look for the proverbial needles in a very large haystack. West Indian cricketers have long gone out of vogue, simply because the team collectively, and players individually, have not merited such positive selection.[35]

While having a degree of understanding for Colin Croft's explanation, other developments have also appeared to influence the numbers of West Indians available to play for English counties. These include the increasing pressures and number of fixtures in the international cricket schedule, and the competition and rewards on offer in the Indian Premier League (IPL), the Bangladesh Premier League (BPL), the Australian domestic Twenty 20 competitions and the Champions League Twenty 20. This suggests that few West Indies players will have the inclination to play county cricket for a considerable length of time during an English season.

An example of a player with West Indian international cricket experience who is scheduled to play a full English season is Ramnaresh Sarwan. After falling out of favour with the WICB, disillusioned with the politics of West Indies cricket, and with no anticipated commitments to other tournaments, Sarwan signed up to play for Leicestershire in the 2012 English domestic season. Leicestershire's chief executive, Mike Siddall, expressed his satisfaction with club's new acquisition by stating that, 'We wanted to sign an experienced overseas batsman and he (Sarwan) certainly fits the bill. He has an impressive test record and his availability to play all forms of the game is an added bonus.'[36]

While the general tide of disengagement with cricket by young people of Caribbean descent and other social backgrounds is a present day reality, initiatives have been developed in Britain in an attempt to reverse this trend. Launched in 2005, The Chance to Shine campaign aims to 'bring competitive cricket, and its educational benefits, back to at least a third of the country's state schools initially over a ten year period.'[37]

The campaign received some proceeds from the 2010 film, Fire in Babylon, which explored the social and political legacy of the 1970s/1980s West Indies cricket team. A short film of Chance to Shine's work, which introduces the DVD version of Fire in Babylon, has helped to raise awareness of the campaign. As Fabian Devlin, Chance to Shine's Head of Communications, explains:

> One of the schemes we are running in the cities, including inner
> city London, Manchester and Birmingham is called StreetChance,
> which gives you the chance to engage in a much quicker game
> rather than a longer version of the game. It's a bit like five-a-side
> football for cricket. Courtney Walsh attended a launch event in
> 2008 in West London and bowled at a couple of the kids there, and
> was so inspired by it that he went and set up his own foundation in
> Jamaica using another version of the game.[38]

The Independent on Sunday newspaper's Happy List 2010, which profiled 100 people 'who make Britain a better and a happier place to live,'[39] included Tony Moody's Lambeth Academy Project in South London. Moody is the director of the project which has Michael Holding as a patron and is the parent body of the community-based Kennington United Cricket Club (KUCC). Moody's work was celebrated as 'Taking cricket from village greens to the inner cities.'[40]

Tony Moody, who arrived in Britain from Jamaica in the 1960s, uses a version of the Jamaican cricket game, catchy shubby, to coach young people who would otherwise avoid playing cricket. The catchy shubby version of cricket offers all participants a sense of involvement by being able to bowl, bat and field in a short period of time.

Since 1995, these cricket activities have attempted to engage young people who attend Moody's sessions in Brixton's Recreational Centre in South London, and appeal to children of Caribbean descent and other social, cultural backgrounds, and non-English speakers of other languages. However, according to Moody, the initiatives inspired by his involvement, are not a remedy for the lack of accessible facilities available for young people to play cricket in Britain's urban city areas:

> What we have done is to bring a kind of injustice to the forefront
> because there are no cricket grounds in my area. Apart from The
> Oval, there is no cricket ground and, especially, no community
> cricket ground. There is nowhere in the Lambeth area to play the
> game properly and I wanted to take that on.[41]

As Steve Stephenson argues, the time to act on re-engaging the Caribbean diaspora with cricket has to be sooner rather than later. Particularly as the network of West Indian cricket clubs in Britain continues to decrease, and the importance of West Indian cricket as an integral part of the diaspora's identity continues to face serious challenges:

At one time in the 1970s and 1980s, there were over 100 West Indian cricket clubs in the UK. Now we are down to about 20 or 30. There are people like me who have tried to maintain the clubs. But, as time has gone on, the third and fourth generation Caribbean generation do not identity themselves with cricket as much. But we try and keep things going because I have a proposal, and I talked to Viv Richards about this, to start a Caribbean cricket supporters' association based here, so we can get tickets and run coaches to matches. We need to restore cricket as part of our identity, which is why I want to start an association. What we don't want, and what I'm afraid of, is in fifteen years time the (West Indies) team come here on tour and there are no Caribbean people in any of the stadiums.[42]

Alongside attempts made to engage the third, fourth and, even, fifth generation of those of Caribbean descent with cricket and, specifically, West Indian cricket, the Caribbean diaspora will continue to be shaped by the changing patterns of West Indian life, self-identification and nationality in Britain. These changes have also contributed to West Indian cricket's decreasing status as a site of Caribbean aspirations in Britain.

A British Labour Force survey reported that by 1998, amongst the black Caribbean population in Britain, 48 per cent of Caribbean men and 34 per cent of women were in an inter-ethnic relationship.[43] For 55 per cent of Caribbean men living with a partner and children under sixteen, and 40 per cent of Caribbean women, that partner was from a different ethnic group.[44]

This evolving trend has resulted in an increasing number of people with mixed identities, of which Caribbean heritage only forms a part. According to figures published by the Office for National Statistics, by 2004, almost nine in ten people (86 per cent) from a Black Caribbean ethnic background described their national identity as British, English, Scottish, Welsh or Irish. Of those from a Black Caribbean background, 83 per cent aged twenty-five to thirty-four were born in the UK.[45]

For the third and fourth generation British born Caribbean diaspora, some of whom are products of inter-ethnic relationships, West Indian cricket is no longer an important source of self-esteem. As the experience of transgenerational black Caribbean solidarity becomes increasingly fragmented, there is limited incentive to associate with the West Indies cricket team and, in particular, a team that is often associated with failure.

For the majority of the current Windrush generation, the West

Indies cricket team no longer fulfils a prominent role in their present-day reality of living in Britain. The current British born generations of Caribbean descent express an identity that is mixed and rarely fixed. It is one where multiple loyalties do not come into conflict with each other and connects with their ethnic origin, family origins and a sense of Britishness.

As a sense of being essentially 'West Indian', and having a pan-Caribbean social, cultural and political outlook decreases in the British-resident Caribbean diaspora, the fortunes of the West Indian cricket team will no longer play an essential role in the projection of the diapora's identity and sense of nationality.

Conclusion

The game of cricket emerged and developed in the British-ruled Caribbean from the early nineteenth century. It was introduced by the elite planter class as a pastime which, through its assumed associated high values, was used to pass on assumed civilised English core values to the rest of the population and distinguish the ruling elite from the rest of colonial society. The importation of cricket also maintained cultural ties with the metropolitan centre of British rule.

Towards the end of the nineteenth century, cricket developed into an activity that was taken up by all the other groups in Caribbean society. Despite the intention of the colonial elite to develop cricket as an exclusive cultural pursuit, levels of participation increased across visible economic, class and race divisions.

In 1928, the West Indies played their first official test match in England as a regional team. In 1950, the West Indies beat England in England for the first time. Two years earlier, the arrival of the Empire Windrush signalled the beginning of mass Caribbean migration to Britain. As the tide of migration increased, some of the diaspora in Britain turned to the West Indies cricket team as a source of self-esteem and ambition.

Although inter-island tensions and differences existed, Barbadians, Guyanese, Jamaicans, Trinidadians and other migrants became collectively self-aware as West Indians in Britain. A sense of Caribbean unity was constructed in exile. As Stuart Hall summarises, 'the island jealousies were also maintained alongside the discovery of a kind of pan-Caribbeanism'.[1] There was a shared experience and identity in coping with migrant life and, in particular, confronting the racial realities of living in Britain.

The West Indies team rapidly became a symbolic link for some Caribbean migrants to their former home and, in this way, cricket acted as a common focus point for migrants from a variety of Caribbean territories, societies and social experiences. During this period, the West Indian team represented an enduring expression of Caribbean unity after the collapse of the West Indian federation. As Hilary Beckles asserts, 'for West Indian residents in England, cricket was their most reliable armoury in the struggle for psychic upliftment, dignity and a general sense of well being and advancement.'[2]

Throughout the 1960s and 1970s, and up to the mid-1990s, some of the first and second-generation Caribbean diaspora responded to a team that was increasingly inspired by a sense of pan-Caribbean nationalist sentiment. The diaspora celebrated a period of West Indian cricket domination from the early 1980s to the mid-1990s and, whether they were passionate cricket fans or not, attached themselves to a symbol of style, skill and success.

Cricket and the West Indies team continued to be a site of self-belief and identity. Cricket grounds in England during West Indian tours, including The Oval in South London and Edgbaston in Birmingham, became assembly points for boisterous West Indian camaraderie and collective expression. West Indian teams collectively responded by taking inspiration from representing the aspirations of the Caribbean diaspora in Britain.

From the mid-1990s, some of the diaspora in Britain responded to the perceived mismanagement of West Indian cricket by the WICB, contractual and sponsorship disputes between the WICB and WIPA, poor results, lacklustre performances by the team, and images of disappointing attendances at matches across the Caribbean region by experiencing a sense of disillusionment with West Indies cricket.

While understanding the need for crowd control, public safety and security, and the trend for commercially driven developments in sport, restrictions on crowd participation, expensive admission prices at English grounds and low availability of pay-on-the-gate tickets have also affected the diaspora's relationship with cricket in Britain. This sense of disengagement has coincided with a third and fourth generation of Caribbean descent who have, largely, disassociated themselves from the game. There is also limited incentive to connect with a West Indian team which is often associated with decline and failure.

Tony Cozier highlighted some of these factors during an edition of the BBC's World Cricket radio programme which was broadcasted by the World Service during the 2007 West Indies tour of England. One of the main items under discussion in the programme was the decreasing numbers of West Indian supporters during West Indian tours in England. Cozier concluded that:

> Back in the 1970s and 1980s, when West Indies came here (to England) they had a great deal of support. One remembers the World Cup finals in 1975 and 1979, especially here at Lord's, with the West Indian spectators sitting on the grass and jumping and shouting and really participating in the cricket. Since then, the ticket prices have gone up astronomically and that is a deterrent. You have to buy your tickets in advance. We don't see the long queues outside the test match grounds that we used to.

The West Indian nature is to wait on the morning of the match to see what the weather is going to be like and so on. In addition, they want to see what the position of the game is like. And if the West Indies are up against it, I don't think they are going to be turning up in their numbers. And, in addition to which, the third and fourth generation West Indians who are here (in Britain) are not as interested in cricket as their parents.[3]

From 1995 to 2010, only four players of Caribbean heritage made England test debuts as cricket continued to struggle to penetrate the imagination of the third and fourth generation Caribbean diaspora. By 2010, the only regular England cricket player of Caribbean descent was Ebony Rainford-Brent, a member of the successful England squad which won the 2009 Women's Cricket World Cup in Australia.

The disconnection with cricket has, arguably, been assisted by the absence of live domestic and international cricket matches covered by free-to-air British terrestrial television channels. Since 2005, live cricket has been relocated to the arena of 'pay-for' sport on television, which makes the game less accessible for a potentially interested audience of younger spectators.

Defeating England at cricket and rejoicing in pan-Caribbean victories over representatives of old Empire has become drastically less important to a diaspora that has evolved a new social, creative, cultural and political identity. It confidently incorporates an identity where being of black Caribbean, mixed race or of Indo-Caribbean descent is no longer mutually exclusive to a sense of Britishness.

The current Caribbean diaspora in Britain have continued to embrace and succeed in other sports, with football, basketball and athletics being the major outlets for their sporting passions and commitment. Cricket is no longer a premier site of expression and identity as there are now multiple avenues of diaspora expression in Britain. These including the creative industries through music, literature, art, fashion, hair and beauty, comedy, television, film, theatre, publishing and digital media. As Mike Phillips vividly summarises:

> What made that a special place and a special period was simply the fact that the relationship between West Indian cricket and West Indian migrants mattered so much. But so much has changed. Today we are no longer driven for yearning for distant refuge and, today, we no longer need a cricket team from overseas to fight our battles or shore up our identity.[4]

The majority of the diaspora no longer reach out to West Indian cricket because the transgenerational connection with their Caribbean ancestral heritage has weakened. They may have pride in their ethnicity and an acknowledgement of their Caribbean background but there is also a sense of remoteness with their Caribbean ancestral origins.

West Indian cricket has lost its once-esteemed status as a social, cultural and political bonding agent for the British-resident Caribbean diaspora. The changing nature of British Caribbean diaspora transgenerational relationships has produced a generation that does not actively seek to attach itself to symbols of pan-Caribbean nationhood.

For most of them, commitment to the affairs of West Indian cricket is seen as an activity of the past and not the present. The majority of people of Caribbean descent, whose forefathers migrated to Britain in the 1950s, 1960s and 1970s, do not reflect an identity which places emphasis on cricket as a source of inspiration.

Their self-awareness doesn't reflect itself through an intimate connection with West Indian cricket. Therefore, the relationship between those of Caribbean descent in Britain and West Indian cricket will continue to be influenced by changing patterns of self-determined identification.

Sustaining distinctive Caribbean cultural and community institutions, including West Indian cricket, sports and social clubs in Britain will become a more serious challenge. There will be fewer individuals with multiple connections to a Caribbean history, which will increase the challenge for families to transmit values and practices associated with Caribbean heritage.[5]

A resurgent West Indian touring team in England, beating England convincingly during a test and one day series, may arouse an increase in interest and optimism in West Indian cricket. In the field of international competitive team sport where cycles of dominance, decline and resurgence can often follow each other, a more successful West Indian cricket team in future years is not completely unimaginable. However, it's difficult to envisage that this would ultimately produce a wide-spread and long-term upsurge of Caribbean diaspora support for West Indian cricket in Britain.

Therefore, with mass Caribbean migration to Britain having ended by the 1960s/1970s, and with the aging first and second generation diaspora slowly passing away or returning to live in the Caribbean; West Indian cricket will continue to struggle to regain its social significance as a barometer of self-worth. It will cease to become a source of common focus as the Caribbean diaspora in Britain continues to experience changing patterns of social and cultural identity.

Footnotes

Introduction

1. David Dabydeen, John Gilmore and Cecily Jones, The Oxford Companion to Black British History (Oxford, 2007), p.155
2. Michael Manley, A History of West Indian Cricket (London, 1988), p.v
3. Hilary McD Beckles, The Development of West Indies Cricket: The Age of Nationalism, Vol. 1 (Jamaica, 1998), p.87
4. Derek Pringle, 'Windies fans in state of trauma', The Independent newspaper website, 13 March 1999, pp.2-3: http://www.independent.co.uk/sport/cricket-w-indies-fans-in-state-of-trauma-1080303.html
5. Frank Keating, Sports Writer's Eye (London, 1989), p.57

Chapter One

1. Hilary McD Beckles, The Development of West Indies Cricket: The Age of Nationalism, Vol. 1 (Jamaica, 1998), p.7
2. Clem Seecharan, Muscular Learning: Cricket and Education in the Making of the British West Indies at the End of the 19th Century (Jamaica, 2006), p.5
3. Brian Stoddart, 'Cricket and colonialism in the English-speaking Caribbean to 1914: towards a cultural analysis', in Hilary McD Beckles and Brian Stoddart (eds), Liberation Cricket: West Indies cricket culture (Manchester, 1995), p.14
4. Michael Manley, A History of West Indian Cricket (London, 1988), p.20
5. CLR James, Beyond a Boundary (London, 2005), p.66
6. Hilary McD Beckles, The Development of West Indies Cricket: The Age of Nationalism, Vol. 1 (Jamaica, 1998), p.7
7. Simon Lister, Supercat – The Authorised biography of Clive Lloyd, (Bath, 2007), p.30
8. Hilary McD Beckles, A History of Barbados: From Amerindian settlement to nation-state (Cambridge, 1990), p.147
9. Ibid., p.148
10. Hilary McD Beckles, A Nation Imagined – The First West Indies Test Team. The 1928 tour (Jamaica, 2003), p.10
11. John Major, More Than a Game: The Story of Cricket's Early Years (London, 2007), p.205

12. Michael Manley, A History of West Indian Cricket (London, 1988), p.21

13. Hilary McD Beckles (ed), The First West Indies Cricket Tour. Canada and the United States in 1886 with The Tour of the West Indian Cricketers August and September 1886, 'A Memory' by One of Them by L.R.Fyfe (Jamaica, 2006), p.18

14. Frank Birbalsingh, The Rise of West Indian Cricket: From colony to Nation (Antigua, 1996), p.156

15. Onyekachi Wambu, Empire Windrush: Fifty Years of Writing About Black Britain (London, 1998), p.20

16. Peter Fryer, Staying Power: The History of Black People in Britain (London, 1984), p.372

17. David Dabydeen, John Gilmore and Cecily Jones, The Oxford Companion to Black British History (Oxford, 2007), p.397

18. Ibid., p.466

19. Andrea Levy, Small Island (London, 2004), pp.156-157

20. Catherine Hall, 'What is a West Indian?' In Bill Schwarz (ed), West Indian intellectuals in Britain (Manchester, 2003), p.34

21. Stuart Hall, 'Politics of Identity', in Terence Ranger, Yunas Samad and Ossie Stuart (eds), Culture, Identity and Politics (Aldershot, 1996), p.130

22. Sam Selvon, 'Three into One Can't Go – East Indian, Trinidadian, West Indian', in Dr. David Dabydeen and Brinsley Samaroo (eds), India in the Caribbean (London, 1987), p.16

23. Mike Phillips and Trevor Phillips, Windrush. The Irresistible Rise of Multi-Racial Britain (London, 1998), p.14

24. Ibid., p.16

25. VS Naipaul, The Middle Passage (London, 1969), p.44

26. Michael Manley, A History of West Indian Cricket (London, 1988), p.93

27. Clyde Walcott with Brian Scovell, Sixty Years on the Back Foot: The Cricketing Life of Sir Clyde Walcott, (London, 1999), p.33

28. Clyde Walcott, interviewed on British Broadcasting Corporation (BBC) Sporting Witness radio programme, 'Calypso Cricketers'. Broadcast on BBC World Service, September 2011

29. Mike Phillips and Trevor Phillips, Windrush. The Irresistible Rise of Multi-Racial Britain (London, 1998), pp.101-102

30. Ibid., p.95

31. The Times newspaper cricket correspondent, 'The Second Test Match: Great Win for the West Indies', The Times, 30 June 1950, p.4

32. Stuart Hall, 'Calypso Kings', Guardian newspaper website, 28 June 2002, p.2: http://www.guardian.co.uk/culture/2002/jun/28/ nottinghillcarnival2002.nottinghillcarnival

33. The Times newspaper cricket correspondent, 'The Second Test Match: Great Win for the West Indies', The Times, 30 June 1950, p.4

34. Vijay P. Kumar, Cricket, Lovely, Cricket. West Indies v England 1950. 50th Anniversary Tribute (New York, 2000), p.127

35. David Dabydeen, John Gilmore and Cecily Jones, The Oxford Companion to Black British History (Oxford, 2007), p.466

36. Michael Melford, 'Blue Skies and Calypsos Greet West Indians', Daily Telegraph, 15th April 1957, p.4

37. Lambeth Services, The Voice newspaper and South London Press, Forty Winters On: Memories of Britain's post-war Caribbean immigrants (London, 1988), p.13

38. Mike Phillips and Trevor Phillips, Windrush. The Irresistible Rise of Multi-Racial Britain (London, 1999), p.121

39. Sam Selvon, The Lonely Londoners (London, 2006), p.126

40. Interview with Mike Phillips by Colin Babb, 12 May 2011

41. Interview with Paul Morrison by Colin Babb, 15 February 2012

42. Paul Morrison, 'Declarations of Independence', The Guardian newspaper website, 29 April 2007, p.2: http://www.guardian.co.uk/film/movie/97032/wondrous.oblivion

43. Interview with Louis Mahoney by Colin Babb, 1 March 2012

44. Simon Lister, Supercat – The Authorised biography of Clive Lloyd (Bath, 2007), p.162

45. Michael Manley, A History of West Indian Cricket, (London, 1988), p.158

46. CLR James, Beyond a Boundary (London, 2005), p.345

47. Hilary McD Beckles, An Area of Conquest: Popular Democracy and West Indies Cricket Supremacy (Jamaica, 1994), p.32

48. Ray Goble and Keith A.P. Sandiford, 75 Years of West Indies Cricket: 1928-2003 (London, 2004), pp.508-510

49. David Dabydeen, John Gilmore and Cecily Jones, The Oxford Companion to Black British History (Oxford, 2007), p.219

50. Ibid., p.219

51. Ian Wooldridge, Cricket, lovely, Cricket: The West Indies Tour 1963 (London, 1963), p.30

52. Ibid., p.30

53. Conrad Hunte, Playing to Win (London, 1971), p.89

54. Interview with Harwood Williams by Colin Babb, 23 March 2012

55. Gary Younge, Who Are We - And Should It Matter in the 21st Century? (London, 2011), p.19

56. Gary Younge, No Place Like Home: A Black Briton's Journey Through The American South (London, 2000), p.7

57. Interview with Rodney Hinds by Colin Babb, 25 January 2012

Chapter Two

1. Dickie Bird, My Autobiography, (London, 1997), p.72

2. Viv Anderson, 'History is Not Always Made With Grand Gestures', in United Colours of Football 4 (London, 2003), p.8

3. James Corbett, England Expects: A History of the England Football Team, (London, 2006), p.362

4. Cass Pennant, Cass, (London, 2002), Introduction

5. Simon Lister, Supercat – The Authorised biography of Clive Lloyd (Bath, 2007), p.107

6. Garry Sobers, My Autobiography (London, 2002), p.262

7. David Tossell, Tony Greig: A Reappraisal of English Cricket's Most Controversial Captain (Brighton, 2011), p.145

8. Tony Greig, My Story, (London, 1980), pp.89-90

9. David Tossell, Grovel, The Story and Legacy of the Summer of 1976 (Studley, 2007), p.71

10. Viv Richards, Hitting Across the Line (London, 1991), p.98

11. Nation On Film, 'The 1976 tour - on and off the pitch', British Broadcasting Corporation (BBC) website, p.4: http://www.bbc.co.uk/nationonfilm/topics/cricket_1976/background.shtml

12. Sir Vivian Richards, Viv Richards: The Definitive Autobiography (London, 2001), p.127

13. Ian Botham, Head On - Ian Botham: The Autobiography (London, 2007), p.262

14. Hilary McD Beckles, The Development of West Indies Cricket: The Age of Nationalism, Vol. 1 (Jamaica, 1998), p.86

15. Mark Marqusee, Anyone but England (London, 1998), p.252

16. Viv Richards, Hitting Across the Line (London, 1991), p.188

17. Vic Marks, 'The power and the glory', Observer newspaper website, 4 March 2007, p.6: http://www.guardian.co.uk/sport/2007/mar/04/cricket.features3

18. Lord Scarman, The Scarman Report: The Brixton Disorders, 10-12 April 1981 (London, 1982), p.196

19. David Dabydeen, John Gilmore and Cecily Jones, The Oxford Companion to Black British History (Oxford, 2007), p.342

20. Michael Holding, No Holding Back: The Autobiography (London, 2010), p.181

21. Gordon Greenidge, Gordon Greenidge: The Man in the Middle (Newton Abbot, 1980), p.49

22. Stevan Riley, Fire in Babylon film (Revolver Entertainment, London 2011)

23. David Tossell, Grovel, The Story and Legacy of the Summer of 1976 (Studley, 2007), p.108

24. Interview with Bill Morris by Colin Babb, 18 August 2011

25. Lambeth Services, The Voice newspaper and South London Press, Forty Winters On: Memories of Britain's post-war Caribbean immigrants (London, 1988), p.43

26. John Woodcock, 'Miller Certain of First Test Cap in the Hope That Ball Will Turn', The Times, 12 August 1976, p.6

27. David Tossell, Grovel, The Story and Legacy of the Summer of 1976, (Studley, 2007), p.201

28. Jack Williams, Cricket and Race (Oxford, 2001), p.131

29. Interview with Ezekel Gray (The Man Ezeke) by Colin Babb, 11 March 2012

30. Interview with Steve Stephenson by Colin Babb, 12 February 2012

31. Michael Melford, 'England slacken grip and West Indies hit back hard', Daily Telegraph, 29th July 1980, p.26

32. England v The West Indies. 1950-1976. 1973, The Oval, Clive Lloyd's 100. (BBC Radio Collection audio cassette set)

33. Simon Lister, Supercat – The Authorised biography of Clive Lloyd (Bath, 2007), p.82

34. Dickie Bird, My Autobiography (London, 1997), p.284

35. Morris OJ, Lord Bill, interviewed on British Broadcasting Corporation (BBC) Archive Hour radio programme, 'When The Oval was ours'. Broadcast on BBC Radio 4, August 2004

36. Interview with Colin Hutton by Colin Babb, 15 March 2012

37. Interview with Bill Morris by Colin Babb, 18 August 2011

38. Interview with Steve Stephenson by Colin Babb, 12 February 2012

39. Interview with Steve Stephenson by Colin Babb, 12 February 2012

40. Interview with Earle Robinson by Colin Babb, 10 February 2012

41. Adrian Turner, 'Playing Away' reviewed, Radio Times website, p.1: http://www.radiotimes.com/servlet_film/com.icl.beeb.rtfilms.client.simp leSearchServlet?frn=12988&searchTypeSelect=5

42. Caryl Phillips, 'The Summer of Broken Boundaries' New Statesmen website, 26 May 2011, p.1: http://www.newstatesman.com/sport/2011/05/cricket-team-west-british

43. Horace Ove, Playing Away (Channel 4 films, London 1986)

44. Horace Ove, Playing Away (Channel 4 films, London 1986)

45. Roland Butcher and Brigette Lawrence, Rising to the Challenge, (London, 1989), pp.64-65

46. Tom Fordyce, 'English cricket's blackout', British Broadcasting Corporation (BBC) website, 22 May 2007, p.2: http://news.bbc.co.uk/sport1/hi/cricket/6650641.stm

47. Interview with Gladstone Small by Colin Babb, 23 November 2011

48. England and Wales Cricket Board (ECB) media release, 'ECB appoint Sir Bill Morris', England and Wales Cricket Board website, 6 October 2004, p.1: http://www.ecb.co.uk/ecb/about-ecb/media-releases/ chairman-hails-decision,2487,EN.html

Chapter Three

1. Hilary McD Beckles, The Development of West Indies Cricket: The Age of Globalization, Vol.2 (Jamaica, 1998), p.7

2. Ibid., p.8

3. Brian Scovell, Brian Lara: Cricket's Troubled Genius (Stroud, Gloucestershire, 2007), p.129-130

4. Vic Marks, 'The power and the glory', The Observer newspaper website, 4 March 2007, p.2: http://www.guardian.co.uk/sport/2007/mar/04/cricket.features3

5. Interview with Professor Clem Seecharan by Colin Babb, 18 August 2011

6. Reliance International Cricket Council (ICC) Rankings, The ICC website, 12 March 2012: http://icc-cricket.yahoo.net/match_zone/test_predictor.php

7. Steven Lynch (ed), The Wisden Book of Test Cricket 2000-2009 (London, 2010), p.410

8. Mike Atherton, 'Precious bond broken in West Indies cricket', Times newspaper website, 28 May 2009, p.1: http://www.timesonline.co.uk/ tol/sport/columnists/mike_atherton/article6374339.ece

9. Frank Birbalsingh, The Rise of West Indian Cricket: From colony to Nation (Antigua, 1996), p.229

10. Jack Williams, Cricket and Race (Oxford, 2001), p.132

11. Marylebone Cricket Club, Lord's. The Home of Cricket: 2011 ticket application brochure (London, 2010), p.7

12. Sir Vivian Richards, Viv Richards: The Definitive Autobiography (London, 2001), p.143

13. Interview with Eaton Gordon by Colin Babb, 15 February 2012

14. Wisden Almanak match report, Fourth Test, West Indies v England, 1993-94. ESPN cricinfo website: http://www.espncricinfo.com/ci/content/story/153212.html

15. Ben Dirs, Everywhere we went: England's Barmy Army (London, 2011), p.159

16. Interview with Mike Phillips by Colin Babb, 12 May 2011

17. Mihir Bose, 'The Big Interview: Rick Parry', Evening Standard, 24 March 2011, p.66

18. 'Manchester United boss Sir Alex Ferguson believes television has too much power over English football', British Broadcasting Corporation (BBC) website, 26 September 2011, p.1: http://www.bbc.co.uk/sport/0/football/15059636

19. David Hopps, 'England lose the generation game as black Britons abandon tradition', Guardian newspaper website, 21 July 2004, p.3: http://www.guardian.co.uk/sport/2004/jul/21/cricket.comment1

20. Rodney Hinds, Black Lions: A history of black players in English football (Cheltenham, 2006), p.189

21. Ibid., p.189

22. 'Man Utd fan Howard Hobson guilty of racial abuse', British Broadcasting Corporation (BBC) website, 8 February 2012, p.2: http://www.bbc.co.uk/news/uk-england-manchester-16950765

23. David Hytner, 'Theo Walcott signs new long-term deal with Arsenal', Guardian newspaper website, 8 May 2009, p.1: http://www.guardian.co.uk/football/2009/may/08/arsenal-theo-walcott-new-contract

24. Tom Fordyce, 'English cricket's blackout', British Broadcasting Corporation (BBC) website, 22 May 2007, p.3: http://news.bbc.co.uk/sport1/hi/cricket/6650641.stm

25. The Sunday Times Sport Rich List 2011, 'The Richest 100 Sportsmen in Britain and Ireland', The Sunday Times, 15 May 2011, p.3

26. Interview with Rodney Hinds by Colin Babb, 25 January 2012

27. Interview with Paul Weekes by Colin Babb, 5 May 2011

28. Interview with Lord Bill Morris by Colin Babb, 18 August 2011

29. 'Toby Radford hoping to revive West Indies', British Broadcasting Corporation (BBC) website, 13 January 2012, pp.1-2: http://www.bbc.co.uk/sport/0/cricket/16450320

30. Simon Wilde, 'Michael Carberry on the verge of remarkable turnaround', Sunday Times website, 24 January 2010, p.1: http://www.timesonline.co.uk/tol/sport/cricket/article6999737.ece

31. Interview with Alex Tudor by Colin Babb, 5 March 2012

32. Interview with Earle Robinson by Colin Babb, 10 February 2012

33. Gordon Ross (ed), Playfair Cricket Annual 1980 (London, 1980), pp.1-240

34. Matt Thacker (ed), The Cricketer's Who's Who 2011 (London, 2011), pp.1-672

35. Colin Croft, 'West Indians Playing in English County Cricket are So Few!' The Professional Cricketers' Association (PCA) website, p.1: http://www.thepca.co.uk/west-indians-playing-in-english-county-cricket-are-so-few.html

36. 'Leicestershire seal Ramnaresh Sarwan deal', British Broadcasting Corporation (BBC) website, 10 February 2012, p.1: http://www.bbc.co.uk/sport/0/cricket/16980199

37. The Campaign, The Chance to Shine website, 2011: http://www.chancetoshine.org/about/campaign

38. Interview with Fabian Devlin by Colin Babb, 13 March 2012

39. James Burgess, The IoS Happy List 2010 - the 100, The Independent on Sunday newspaper website, Sunday 25 April 2010, p.1: http://www.independent.co.uk/news/people/news/the-iiosi-happy-list-2010--the-100-1953745.html

40. Ibid., pp.9-10

41. Interview with Tony Moody by Colin Babb, 25 January 2012

42. Interview with Steve Stephenson by Colin Babb, 12 February 2012

43. Lucinda Platt, Ethnicity and Family. Relationships within and between ethnic groups: An analysis using the Labour Force Survey (Essex, 1998), p.7

44. Ibid., p.7

45. Office for National Statistics (ONS) online, Ethnicity and Identity - Census, April 2001, (2006), p.1: http://www.statistics.gov.uk/cci/nugget.asp?id=459

Conclusion

1. Stuart Hall, 'Politics of Identity', in Terence Ranger, Yunas Samad and Ossie Stuart (eds), Culture, Identity and Politics (Aldershot, 1996), p.130

2. Hilary McD Beckles, An Area of Conquest: Popular Democracy and West Indies Cricket Supremacy (Jamaica, 1994), p.51

3. Tony Cozier, interviewed on British Broadcasting Corporation (BBC) World Cricket radio programme item, 'Where are the West Indian fast bowlers and where are their fans?' Broadcast on BBC World Service, June 2007

4. Mike Phillips, presenter of British Broadcasting Corporation (BBC) Archive Hour radio programme, 'When The Oval was ours'. Broadcast on BBC Radio 4, August 2004

5. Lucinda Platt, Ethnicity and Family. Relationships within and between ethnic groups: An analysis using the Labour Force Survey (Essex, 1998), pp.7-8

Bibliography

Primary sources

Atherton, Mike, Precious bond broken in West Indies cricket, Times newspaper website, 2009, p.1: http://www.timesonline.co.uk/tol/sport/columnists/mike_atherton/article6374339.ece

Bose, Mihir, The Big Interview: Rick Parry, Evening Standard, 24 March 2011

Burgess, James, The IoS Happy List 2010 - the 100, The Independent on Sunday newspaper website, Sunday 25 April 2010, p.1: http://www.independent.co.uk/news/people/news/the-iiosi-happy-list-2010--the-100-1953745.html

Chance to Shine, The Campaign, The Chance to Shine website, 2011: http://www.chancetoshine.org/about/campaign

Cozier, Tony, interviewed on British Broadcasting Corporation (BBC) World Cricket radio programme item, 'Where are the West Indian fast bowlers and where are their fans?' Broadcast on BBC World Service, June 2007

Croft, Colin, West Indians Playing in English County Cricket are So Few! The Professional Cricketers' Association (PCA) website, p.1: http://www.thepca.co.uk/west-indians-playing-in-english-county-cricket-are-so-few.html

Devlin, Fabian, Head of Communications, Chance to Shine campaign. Interviewed by Colin Babb on 13 March 2012

England and Wales Cricket Board (ECB) media release, ECB appoint Sir Bill Morris, England and Wales Cricket Board website, 2004, p.1:

http://www.ecb.co.uk/ecb/about-ecb/media-releases/chairman-hails-decision,2487,EN.html

England v The West Indies. 1950-1976. 1973, The Oval, Clive Lloyd's 100. (BBC Radio Collection audio cassette set) 1990

Fordyce, Tom, English cricket's blackout, British Broadcasting Corporation (BBC) website, 2007, p.2: http://news.bbc.co.uk/sport1/hi/cricket/6650641.stm

Gordon, Eaton, Deputy Sports Development Officer and Warwickshire Cricket Board Community Officer. Chance To Shine Manager and Head Coach of Handsworth Cricket Club in Birmingham. Interviewed by Colin Babb on 15 February 2012

Gray, Ezeke (The Man Ezeke), DJ, Entertainer and Musician. Writer and performer of 'Whose Grovelling Now?' Interviewed by Colin Babb on 11 March 2012

Hall, Stuart, Calypso Kings, Guardian newspaper website, 2002, p.2: http://www.guardian.co.uk/culture/2002/jun/28/nottinghillcarnival2002.nottinghillcarnival

Hinds, Rodney, Sports Editor, The Voice newspaper. Interviewed by Colin Babb on 25 January 2012

Hopps, David, England lose the generation game as black Britons abandon tradition, Guardian newspaper website, 2004, p.3: http://www.guardian.co.uk/sport/2004/jul/21/cricket.comment1

Hutton, Colin, Former Crowd Control Police Sergeant at The Oval cricket ground. Interviewed by Colin Babb on 15 March 2012

Hytner, David, Theo Walcott signs new long-term deal with Arsenal, Guardian newspaper website, 2009, p.1: http://www.guardian.co.uk/football/2009/may/08/arsenal-theo-walcott-new-contract

Mahoney, Louis, Actor and club cricketer. Interviewed by Colin Babb on 1 March 2012

Manchester United boss Sir Alex Ferguson believes television has too much power over English football, British Broadcasting Corporation (BBC) website, 26 September 2011, p.1: http://www.bbc.co.uk/sport/0/football/15059636

Man Utd fan Howard Hobson guilty of racial abuse, British Broadcasting Corporation (BBC) website, 8 February 2012, p.2: http://www.bbc.co.uk/news/uk-england-manchester-16950765

Marks, Vic, The power and the glory, Observer newspaper website, 2007, p.2: http://www.guardian.co.uk/sport/2007/mar/04/cricket.features3

Marylebone Cricket Club, Lord's. The Home of Cricket: 2011 ticket application brochure, (MCC) 2010

Melford, Michael, Blue Skies and Calypsos Greet West Indians, Daily Telegraph newspaper, 15 April 1957

Melford, Michael, England Slacken Grip and West Indies Hit Back Hard, Daily Telegraph newspaper, 29 July 1980

Moody, Tony, Cricket coach and Director of the Lambeth Cricket Academy. Interviewed by Colin Babb on 25 January 2012

Morris OJ, Lord Bill, Independent non-executive director of the England and Wales Cricket Board (ECB). Interviewed by Colin Babb on 18 August 2011

Morris OJ, Lord Bill, interviewed on British Broadcasting Corporation (BBC) Archive Hour radio programme, 'When The Oval was ours'. Broadcast on BBC Radio 4, August 2004

Morrison, Paul, Declarations of Independence, The Guardian newspaper website, 29 April 2007, p.2: http://www.guardian.co.uk/film/movie/97032/wondrous.oblivion

Morrison, Paul, Writer and director of film, Wondrous Oblivion. Interviewed by Colin Babb on 15 February 2012

Nation on Film, The 1976 tour-on and off the pitch, British Broadcasting Corporation (BBC) website, p.1: http://www.bbc.co.uk/nationonfilm/topics/cricket_1976/background.shtml

Office for National Statistics (ONS) online, Ethnicity and Identity - Census, April 2001, 2006, p.1: http://www.statistics.gov.uk/cci/nugget.asp?id=459

Phillips, Caryl, The Summer of Broken Boundaries, New Statesmen website, 26 May 2011, p.1: http://www.newstatesman.com/sport/2011/05/cricket-team-west-british

Phillips, Mike, Academic, broadcaster and writer. Interviewed by Colin Babb on 11 May 2011

Phillips, Mike, presenter of British Broadcasting Corporation (BBC) Archive Hour radio programme, 'When The Oval was ours'. Broadcast on BBC Radio 4, August 2004

Pringle, Derek, Windies fans in state of trauma, The Independent newspaper website, 13 March 1999, p.2-3: http://www.independent.co.uk/sport/cricket-w-indies-fans-in-state-of-trauma-1080303.html

Reliance International Cricket Council (ICC) rankings, The ICC website, 12 March 2012: http://icc-cricket.yahoo.net/match_zone/test_predictor.php

Robinson, Earle, Cultural archivist and Leicester Caribbean Cricket Club trustee. Interviewed by Colin Babb on 10 February 2012

Scovell, Brian, Brian Lara: Cricket's Troubled Genius, (Stadia) 2007

Seecharan, Professor Clem, Head of Caribbean Studies at London Metropolitan University, academic and cricket writer. Interviewed by Colin Babb on 30 November 2011

Small, Gladstone, Professional Cricketers'Association (PCA) ambassador. Former professional cricket player for Warwickshire and England. Interviewed by Colin Babb on 23 November 2011

Stephenson, Steve, Caribbean community leader, lecturer and chairman of the Victoria Mutual Caribbean Cup cricket competition. Interviewed by Colin Babb on 12 February 2012

The Sunday Times Sport Rich List 2011, The Richest 100 Sportsmen in Britain and Ireland, Sunday Times newspaper, 15 May 2011

The Times cricket correspondent, The Second Test Match: Great Win for the West Indies, The Times newspaper, 30 June 1950

Toby Radford hoping to revive West Indies, British Broadcasting Corporation (BBC) website, 13 January 2012: http://www.bbc.co.uk/sport/0/cricket/16450320

Tudor, Alex, Cricket coach. Former professional cricket player for Surrey, Essex and England. Interviewed by Colin Babb on 5 March 2012

Turner, Adrian, review of Playing Away, Radio Times website, p.1: http://www.radiotimes.com/servlet_film/com.icl.beeb.rtfilms.client.simpleSearchServlet?frn=12988&searchTypeSelect=5

Walcott, Clyde, interviewed on British Broadcasting Corporation (BBC) Sporting Witness radio programme, 'Calypso Cricketers'. Broadcast on BBC World Service, September 2011

Weekes, Paul, Cricket coach. Former professional cricket player for Middlesex. Interviewed by Colin Babb on 5 May 2011

Wilde, Simon, Michael Carberry on the verge of remarkable turnaround, Sunday Times website, 2010, p.1: http://www.timesonline.co.uk/tol/sport/cricket/article6999737.ece

Williams, Harwood, Chairman of the Leeds Caribbean Cricket Club. Interviewed by Colin Babb on 23 March 2012

Wisden Almanak match report, Fourth Test, West Indies v England, 1993-94. ESPN cricinfo website: http://www.espncricinfo.com/ci/content/story/153212.html

Woodcock, John, Miller Certain of First Test Cap in the Hope That Ball Will Turn, The Times newspaper, 12 August 1976

Secondary published sources

Anderson, Viv, History is Not Always Made With Grand Gestures, in United Colours of Football 4, (Kick It Out) 2003

Beckles, Hilary McD, A History of Barbados: From Amerindian settlement to nation-state, (Cambridge University Press) 1990

Beckles, Hilary McD, An Area of Conquest: Popular Democracy and West Indies Cricket Supremacy, (Ian Randle Publishers) 1994

Beckles, Hilary McD, A Nation Imagined – The First West Indies Test Team. The 1928 tour, (Ian Randle Publishers) 2003

Beckles, Hilary McD, The Development of West Indies Cricket: The Age of Nationalism, Vol. 1, (The Press University of the West Indies) 1998

Beckles, Hilary McD, The Development of West Indies Cricket: The Age of Globalisation, Vol. 2, (The Press University of the West Indies) 1998

Beckles, Hilary McD (ed), The First West Indies Cricket Tour. Canada and the United States in 1886 with The Tour of the West Indian Cricketers August and September 1886, 'A Memory' by One of Them by L.R.Fyfe (Canoe Press) 2006

Birbalsingh, Frank, The Rise of West Indian Cricket: From colony to Nation, (Hansib) 1996

Bird, Dickie, My Autobiography, (Hodder and Stoughton) 1997

Botham, Ian, Head On - Ian Botham: The Autobiography, (Ebury Press) 2007

Butcher, Roland and Lawrence, Brigette, Rising to the Challenge, (Pelham Books) 1989

Corbett, James, England Expects: A History of the England Football Team, (Aurum Press Ltd) 2006

Dabydeen, David, Gilmore, John and Jones, Cecily, The Oxford Companion to Black British History, (Oxford University Press) 2007

Dirs, Ben, Everywhere we went: England's Barmy Army, (Simon and Schuster) 2011

Fryer, Peter, Staying Power: The History of Black People in Britain, (Pluto Press) 1984

Goble, Ray and Sandiford, Keith A.P, 75 Years of West Indies Cricket: 1928-2003, (Hansib) 2004

Greenidge, Gordon, Gordon Greenidge: The Man in the Middle, (David and Charles) 1980

Greig, Tony, My Story, (Stanley Paul and Co) 1980

Hall, Catherine, What is a West Indian? In West Indian intellectuals in Britain, edited by Bill Schwarz, (Manchester University Press) 2003

Hall, Stuart, Politics of Identity, in Culture, Identity and Politics, edited by Terence Ranger, Yunas Samad and Ossie Stuart, (Avebury) 1996

Hinds, Rodney, Black Lions: A history of black players in English football, (SportsBooks Limited) 2006

Holding, Michael, No Holding Back: The Autobiography, (Weidenfeld & Nicolson) 2010

Hunte, Conrad, Playing to Win, (Hodder and Stoughton) 1971

James, CLR, Beyond A Boundary, (Yellow Jersey Press) 2005

Keating, Frank, Sports Writer's Eye, (Macdonald Queen Anne Press) 1989

Kumar, Vijay P, Cricket, Lovely, Cricket. West Indies v England 1950. 50th Anniversary Tribute (Vijay P. Kumar) 2000

Lambeth Services, The Voice newspaper, South London Press, Forty Winters On: Memories of Britain's post-war Caribbean immigrants (Lambeth Council) 1988

Levy, Andrea, Small Island, (Headline) 2004

Lister, Simon, Supercat – The Authorised biography of Clive Lloyd, (Fairfield Books) 2007

Lynch, Steven (ed), The Wisden Book of Test Cricket 2000-2009 (A & C Black Publishers Ltd) 2010

Major, John, More Than a Game: The Story of Cricket's Early Years, (Harper Collins Publishers) 2007

Manley, Michael, A History of West Indian Cricket, (André Deutsch Limited) 1988

Marqusee, Mark, Anyone but England, (Two Heads Publishing) 1998

Naipaul, VS, The Middle Passage, (Penguin) 1969

Ové, Horace (director), Playing Away DVD, (Channel 4 films) 1986

Pennant, Cass, Cass, (John Blake Publishing) 2002

Phillips, Mike and Phillips, Trevor, Windrush, The Irresistible Rise of Multi-Racial Britain, (HarperCollins) 1998

Phillips, Mike and Phillips, Trevor, Windrush, The Irresistible Rise of Multi-Racial Britain, (HarperCollins) 1999

Platt, Lucinda, Ethnicity and Family. Relationships within and between ethnic groups: An analysis using the Labour Force Survey, (Institute for Social and Economic Research, University of Essex) 1998

Richards, Sir Vivian, Viv Richards: The Definitive Autobiography, (Penguin) 2001

Richards, Viv, Hitting Across the Line, (Headline) 1991

Riley, Stevan (director), Fire in Babylon DVD, (Revolver Entertainment) 2011

Ross, Gordon (ed), Playfair Cricket Annual 1980, (Queen Anne Press) 1980

Scarman, Lord, The Scarman Report: The Brixton Disorders, 10-12 April 1981, (Pelican Books) 1982

Seecharan, Clem, Muscular Learning: Cricket and Education in the Making of the British West Indies at the End of the 19th Century, (Ian Randle Publishers) 2000

Selvon, Sam, The Lonely Londoners, (Penguin) 2006

Selvon, Sam, Three into One Can't Go – East Indian, Trinidadian, West Indian, in India in the Caribbean, edited by Dr. David Dabydeen and Brinsley Samaroo, (Hansib Publishing) 1987

Sobers, Garry, My Autobiography, (Headline) 2002

Stoddart, Brian, Cricket and colonialism in the English-speaking Caribbean to 1914: towards a cultural analysis, in Liberation Cricket: West Indies cricket culture, edited by Hilary McD Beckles and Brian Stoddart, (Manchester University Press) 1995

Thacker, Matt (ed), The Cricketer's Who's Who 2011, (All Out Cricket Ltd) 2011

Tossell, David, Grovel, The Story and Legacy of the Summer of 1976, (Know The Score Books Limited) 2007

Tossell, David, Tony Greig: A Reappraisal of English Cricket's Most Controversial Captain, (Pitch Publishing) 2011

Walcott, Clyde with Scovell, Brian, Sixty Years on the Back Foot: The Cricketing Life of Sir Clyde Walcott, (Victor Gollancz) 1999

Wambu, Onyekachi, Empire Windrush: Fifty Years of Writing about Black Britain, (Weidenfeld & Nicolson) 1998

Williams, Jack, Cricket and Race, (Berg) 2001

Wooldridge, Ian, Cricket, lovely, Cricket: The West Indies Tour 1963, (Robert Hale) 1963

Younge, Gary, No Place Like Home: A Black Briton's Journey Through The American South, (Picador) 2000

Younge, Gary, Who Are We – And Should It Matter in the 21st Century? (Penguin) 2011